CULTURAL PROPERTY ACQUISITIONS

TECHNIQUES AND ISSUES IN CULTURAL RESOURCES MANAGEMENT

Series Editor: Caryn M. Berg

This series is designed to provide practical guidance to the day-to-day practice of cultural resources management through a series of brief guides. Guides are directed at the professional in this field, students in heritage management programs and field schools, and the consumers of CRM work. Manuscripts, proposals, and letters of inquiry should be directed to the series editor at archaeology@lcoastpress.com

Negotiation Basics for Cultural Resource Managers, *Nicholas Dorochoff*

Avoiding Archaeological Disasters: A Risk Management Approach, *Darby Stapp and Julia Longenecker*

Cultural Property Acquisitions: Navigating the Shifting Landscape, *Aimée L. Taberner*

CULTURAL PROPERTY ACQUISITIONS

Navigating the Shifting Landscape

Aimée L. Taberner

Left Coast Press Inc.

Walnut Creek, California

LEFT COAST PRESS, INC.
1630 North Main Street, #400
Walnut Creek, CA 94596
http://www.LCoastPress.com

ISBN 978-1-61132-109-8 hardcover
ISBN 978-1-61132-110-4 paperback
ISBN 978-1-61132-111-1 electronic

Library of Congress Cataloging-in-Publication Data:

Taberner, Aimée L.
Cultural property acquisitions : navigating the shifting landscape / Aimée L. Taberner.
p. cm. — (Techniques and issues in cultural resources management)
Includes bibliographical references and index.
ISBN 978-1-61132-109-8 (hardcover : alk. paper) — ISBN 978-1-61132-110-4 (pbk. : alk. paper) — ISBN 978-1-61132-111-1 (ebook)
1. Museums—Law and legislation—United States. 2. Cultural property—Protection—Law and legislation—United States. 3. Museums—Acquisitions—Government policy—United States. I. Title.
KF4305.T33 2011
344.73'093—dc23
2011025112

Printed in the United States of America

∞™ The paper used in this publication meets the minimum requirements of American National Standard for Information Sciences—Permanence of Paper for Printed Library Materials, ANSI/NISO Z39.48–1992.

Dedication

This publication is dedicated to my parents, Ernest and Laura Phyllis Taberner, in appreciation of their boundless love and support.

Contents

List of Tables*

*Unless otherwise specified, all tables and parts of tables have been created by the author.

Preface

Museum staff—whether new to the field or working with collections for decades—are often overwhelmed by the complexities of acquiring cultural property, particularly antiquities and archaeological material. As an intern at the Harvard Peabody Museum of Archaeology and Ethnology (PMAE), I was surprised to encounter a degree of uncertainty about this, despite the museum's strong track record of ethical collecting and rigorous acquisition policies regarding antiquities. This uncertainty was due in part to the differing perceptions of "legal" and "ethical" collecting. The responses to a survey received from over thirty museums worldwide revealed this varied understanding of what constitutes permissible and moral acquisition was not limited to Harvard. Policies and procedures diverged widely, as did knowledge of and adherence to the legal parameters restricting acquisitions.

This book began as an attempt to operationalize and neutralize Harvard PMAE's approach to acquisitions by providing an overview of applicable law, an agreed-on glossary of terms to facilitate discussion, and procedural recommendations for acquisition review based on industry-accepted best practices. This research continued as my graduate thesis under the direction of faculty at Harvard Law, ensuring that the information and recommendations were based on a solid understanding of common law principles governing property as well as the various foreign and domestic legal means specifically intended to control or otherwise applied to the distribution of cultural property.

My goal has been to provide an unbiased and practical resource for those tasked with navigating the complicated and rapidly changing legal and ethical landscape governing the acquisition of cultural property and archaeological material—a complicated undertaking that entails a significant degree of risk. I hope that this publication contributes to increased stewardship of our world's cultural heritage and protects museums and those working with cultural property.

Acknowledgments

This publication would not have been possible without the intellectual contribution and personal support of Dr. Genevieve Fisher, registrar of PMAE, who gave generously of her time and insight. I also thank Dr. Patricia Capone, associate curator at PMAE, who, with Dr. Fisher, oversaw the initial development of this research. I am grateful for their enthusiasm and collaboration and for the confidence they placed in me.

My internship at PMAE involved the review of collections policies and procedures of dozens of museums from around the world. I am grateful to those museum professionals who responded to my acquisition questionnaire and voiced support for my research topic. I hope that this resource is of assistance to them and to future generations of museum professionals.

It is impossible to mention all resources that were critical to the development of this publication, but three documents stand out as exemplary. These include two publications originating from the United Kingdom, *Combating Illicit Trade: Due Diligence Guidelines for Museums, Libraries and Archives on Collecting and Borrowing Cultural Material*[1] and Paul Roberts's article "Barriers or Bridges? Museums and Acquisitions,"[2] as well as Marie Malaro's *A Legal Primer on Managing Museum Collections.*[3]

I am indebted to Professor Harry S. Martin III (Terry) of the Harvard Law School who generously gave of his time, resources, and knowledge to inform and guide my legal analyses and procedural recommendations during the development of this research for my thesis and who continues to patiently address my questions. Professor Martin's guidance in translating the relevance of legislation and case law to museum practice was invaluable.

In addition, I wish to thank Left Coast Press for publishing this book. The patience and support demonstrated by Mitch Allen, publisher, Caryn Berg, series editor, Carole Bernard, editor, and others is greatly appreciated.

Finally, I am grateful for the many friends and colleagues who aided in the development of this publication, particularly Paul Taberner, Ginna Johnson, Joan Zofnass, David Taberner, Carrie Pinsker, and Sarah Burks. Lastly, this publication would not have been possible without the support and encouragement of my husband, Patrick Guthrie.

Chapter 1

Introduction

In recent years, the following headlines have appeared in local and national newspapers:

- Several Museums May Possess Looted Art; Italian Prosecutors Use Photos Seized from a Convicted Trafficker of Stolen Antiquities to Identify Dozens of Suspect Objects[1]
- Museum Workers Are Called Complicit[2]
- Italy Focuses on a Princeton Curator in an Antiquities Investigation[3]
- Fed Agents Raid California Museums for Looted Artifacts[4]
- Raids Suggest a Deeper Network of Looted Art[5]
- Cleveland Museum of Art Will Return Tainted Antiquities to Italy Wednesday[6]

These are but a few of the many articles focusing on the purported negative impact museum collecting has had, and continues to have, on the archaeological record and cultural patrimony of certain regions, both within and outside the United States. They show museums in a decidedly negative light; as a result of these stories, the public's perception of museums may well be shifting. The voice of the museum community has been largely lost among the allegations of archaeologists, source country representatives, and the media.

Clearly, collecting archaeological and antiquated cultural material entails risk—of financial loss, criminal liability, public disapproval, and damaged relations with source countries and descendent communities. The collecting practices of old are no longer adequate. A greater degree of scrutiny, transparency, and cooperation is expected of museums by all stakeholders. Although the museum community has been proactively and collaboratively addressing this centuries-old and complicated problem for over thirty years by changing their standards of acceptable collecting practices, it is increasingly urgent that museums ensure that policies and practices are in line with current legal requirements and ethical expectations.

Museum professionals are now tasked with determining how changing legislation, legal precedents, negotiated agreements, and federal investigations directly impact their museums and how best to safeguard their museums and themselves in the acquisition process. Understanding this complex landscape is not easy, especially since it is not the primary discipline of most museum staff. The tumultuousness of the situation is understandable given the complexities of the legal landscape governing acquisitions, the extreme and relatively sudden change in the interpretation and application of these laws, as well as the broader discussion of sovereignty, identity politics, and cultural stewardship.

Online and printed resources discussing acquisitions are often highly biased, accusatory, and lacking in practical guidance. Often, these documents reflect the politically charged nature of the debate surrounding the continued destruction of the archaeological record and cultural patrimony in many parts of the world and the alleged role that museums have played in this destruction. Although most museums have legal counsel, these attorneys may not be adequately versed in the unique nature of art, cultural property, or museum law.

Great strides have been made in recent years as professional museum organizations such as the American Association of Museums (AAM) and the Association of Art Museum Directors (AAMD) seek to address the dearth of agreed-on information, by releasing the Report of the AAMD Task Force on the Acquisition of Archaeological Materials and Ancient Art and AAM's Standards Regarding Archaeological Material and Ancient Art. Questions remain as to how museum staff can and should implement these guidelines and standards in ways that work for their particular institutions. Some may argue that these guidelines and standards fail to provide sufficient guidance in explaining or navigating the legal landscape. Indeed, these documents are not comprehensive in their coverage of domestic and foreign law and fail to provide guidance regarding domestic acquisitions. While these documents are helpful resources, they are not law; rather, they are recommendations based in part on law and in part on the organizations' philosophical viewpoints. Museums that adopt these recommendations remain obligated to understand the laws governing their actions and provide adequate guidance to ensure that their staff acts in accordance with legal rules and their institution's unique mission and philosophy.

The objective of this book is to provide unbiased guidance, both practical and implementable, to those tasked with collecting archaeological and antiquated cultural material. It is intended to help these individuals better understand the risks associated with collecting cultural property and archaeological material, particularly pertaining to the legal landscape governing acquisitions, and aid museums in formulating a comprehensive plan to mitigate these risks. Knowledge of the relevant laws and a museum's ethics and mission statements are the keys to developing a sound policy to guide acquisition of cultural property, which can then be operationalized through thoughtful and clearly documented acquisition review procedures. The fundamental tasks of risk assessment and risk management are integral to the process. The information provided in this publication is a compilation of a wide variety of resources, strategies, and best practices available to museums, or created by museums, but reorganized to guide museum staff through the progressive steps needed for a comprehensive policy and procedure for cultural property acquisitions in a user-friendly format.

Determining whether to acquire an object is rarely a risk-free undertaking, especially because of the attention given to the issue by the U.S. government, foreign and domestic courts, foreign countries and originating communities, the press, and the general public. However, potential risk should be weighed against the laudable goal of continued access to these items within museums. The task is to ensure that the acquisition is made in a legally and ethically responsible way that safeguards museums and their staff as well as our global cultural heritage.

At its core, the approach advocated here strongly reaffirms that education and preservation are the fundamental purposes of collecting. Museums may look at the recent events as the latest in a long history of transformation for museums—a continuum wherein the means and methods of achieving those fundamental purposes have evolved. Changing standards of acceptable collecting practice are but one indication of a broader paradigm shift. With the adoption of this philosophical outlook, one can imagine a future where museums play an increasingly relevant role in the lives of their constituents and occupy an integral and cooperative position in the preservation and sharing of both the physical and intellectual aspects of our global cultural heritage. This book takes the position that change is not an obstacle, but rather an opportunity.

Clearly defined and documented collections policies and procedures incorporating an understanding of legal precedent and an institution's individual philosophical and ethical framework are essential to the appearance of accountability and transparency in museums. It is only when these policies are in place, and are acted on, that museums may move beyond the traditional role of stewards of their collections to stewards of our shared global cultural heritage.[7]

Organization

Chapter 2 provides an overview of the legal landscape governing the acquisition of foreign and domestic cultural property. The chapter starts with a brief introduction to common-law principles of personal property, which is followed by the myriad exceptions to these rules as illustrated by specific legislation governing particular types or origins of property.

Chapter 3 has recommendations for crafting a policy to govern the acquisition of cultural property, specifically archaeological material over 100 years old. A list of recommended steps museums may take when crafting a customized policy for their institution is given, as is a summary of the philosophical viewpoints and organizational affiliations that may influence a museum's collecting policies and practices. Specific questions are listed to aid museums in formulating a customized policy developed to meet their specific needs.

Chapter 4 offers recommendations regarding preliminary steps a museum must take to successfully implement its policy and provides an overview of the procedural recommendations outlined in Chapters 5, 6, and 7.

Chapter 5 summarizes the procedural steps necessary for reviewing the legality and ethicality of an acquisition, including recommendations regarding documentation collection and assessment, analysis of provenance (history of an object including ownership, publication, display, conservation, etc.), provenience (object's archaeological record, including exactly when, where, how, by whom, and in what context the object was found), and legal status as well as additional due diligence procedures. Suggestions for protecting the institution and its staff during and after the acquisition process are integrated into Chapter 5.

To simplify organization, the procedural review of the basic criteria for acquisitions, which primarily focuses on the legal review of the acquisition, is covered in two chapters: Chapter 6 is about domestic cultural property and Chapter 7 covers foreign property.

Chapter 8 provides examples of museums that have successfully gone beyond law and policy to the realm of public relations and education and summarizes my reflections on the future of museum collecting.

SCOPE AND LIMITATIONS

This publication is intended as a guide for the acquisition of antiquities. For purposes of this book, antiquities are considered cultural material over 100 years old, often of an archaeological nature. There are many types of material that satisfy the definition above but are outside the scope of this book. These exclusions are listed in Table 1.1. Items classified in Table 1.1 have additional specific legal and procedural requirements beyond the scope of this book. Acquisitions from these categories should be subject to the same thoughtful scrutiny as other antiquities, but a museum should be aware of the additional legal and cultural issues

Table 1.1: Cultural Property Types Outside the Scope of This Book

Material originating from underwater sites and shipwrecks	Generally speaking, the legal status of these items has likely already been established prior to arrival at a museum. However, if obtained from a relatively recent underwater discovery, legal counsel should be sought to determine if other parties hold a legal interest in the material. For more information, refer to the 2001 UNESCO Convention on the Protection of the Underwater Cultural Heritage and the U.S. Abandoned Shipwreck Act (Pub.L. 100-298; 43 U.S.C. 2101-2106) of 1998.
Human remains	Although covered in general terms through the Native American Graves Protection and Repatriation Act, the report does not specifically address the acquisition of human remains. Common law holds that "there is no property right in the body of a deceased person."[1] While the legal and ethical ramifications of the acquisition, collection, and care of human remains are outside the scope of this book, it is essential that a museum draft a specific policy to guide staff and museum boards.
Nazi-era material	Items created before 1946 and acquired by the museum after 1932 that may have been in continental Europe between 1932 and 1946, with either an indication of transferred ownership or a gap in provenance during this period, may pose specific issues for a museum. However, well-accepted and articulated policies and procedures are already in place for working with this property, both in terms of acquisitions, collections review, and claims. The procedural guidelines in Chapter 5 do not specifically cover review processes specifically for Nazi-era material. See the Nazi-era provenance information provided on the American Association of Museums website < http://www.aam-us.org/museumresources/prov/index.cfm > for more information.
Endangered species and items incorporating wildlife	Additional procedural considerations for items containing endangered animals or flora are not incorporated in the review process outlined in Chapter 5. See the following for more information on laws protecting plants and wildlife: The Lacey Act, Convention on International Trade in Endangered Species of Wild Fauna and Flora, Endangered Species Act, Marine Mammal Protection Act, Migratory Bird Treaty Act, Bald and Golden Eagle Protection Act, The Wild Exotic Bird Conservation Act, Asian Elephant Conservation Act, African Elephant Conservation Act, and the Antarctic Conservation Act.
Other issues affecting the general quality or completeness of title	These include copyright issues and other restrictions, unresolved claims on bequeathed material, etc., that are also outside of the scope of this book. Marie Malaro's *A Legal Primer on Managing Museum Collections*[2] should be referred to for general questions regarding title as well as for more information on the categories of material listed above.

involved. Additional resources for these types of material are provided in Appendix F.

This book does not provide legal advice; rather, I strive to offer a useful resource to museum staff and hope the recommendations enable museum administrations, in consultation with their governing boards and legal counsel, to address acquisition issues in a proactive manner. Museums should consult legal counsel when drafting an acquisition policy, before implementing procedures, and for professional guidance regarding all possibly contentious acquisitions.

This publication focuses on what can be done—in a proactive manner that shows museums in a positive light—to avoid, to the greatest extent possible, controversial situations regarding acquisitions of cultural property, but does not provide instruction for responding to future claims.

Chapter 2

The Rapidly Changing Legal Landscape Governing Museum Acquisitions of Cultural Property

The number of laws restricting the acquisition of cultural property—both in the United States and abroad—has increased rapidly, particularly since the 1970s, and the interpretation and application of these laws have changed significantly, even in the last decade. Those tasked with acquiring cultural property on behalf of their institution may find understanding the complexities of this rapidly shifting legal landscape challenging. Given the negative press the purportedly illegal and unethical collection of antiquities by museums has received in recent years and the recent application of laws that criminalize the acquisition of items defined as stolen by sweeping foreign patrimony laws, the task of collecting poses significant risk—both for museums as well as for staff acting on a museum's behalf.

This chapter provides museum staff with an introduction to the laws governing the acquisition of antiquated cultural property,[1] beginning with a brief introduction to the primary common-law principles governing personal property (movable, tangible items) as they relate to museum acquisitions. This section also outlines the various types of property that pose exceptions to these general principles, which are governed by specific rules further restricting ownership, transport, excavation, and/or title transfer.

Summaries are then given for the legislation, regulations, conventions, agreements, and treaties that govern these exceptional property types. Acquisitions fall into two distinct categories: items originating within the United States and those originating outside the United States. The legal frameworks governing U.S. and international acquisitions are substantially different. Therefore, summaries of applicable legislation, conventions, and polices, as well as guidelines for due diligence and acceptable documentation, are given separately for both categories of objects.

Basic Principles of Common Law Relating to Acquisitions of Personal Property

A basic understanding of common-law principles governing the transfer of property is helpful for those responsible for ensuring the legality of acquisitions. In essence, if the museum obtains an item that was previously stolen, or possibly taken without permission from another's property, the museum will not obtain good title to the item. The common-law *nemo dat* rule (or "Nemo dat quod non habet" meaning "no one can give a better title than he has")[2] generally prevails. This rule is enforced through Section 2–403 of the Uniform Commercial Code, which asserts that if the item is acquired from someone lacking legal ownership, the acquirer will not receive title. Title remains with the last legal owner of the item who retains the right to reclaim the property either through replevin (return of the property itself), or, lacking that, monetary damages. To balance the rights of owners and good-faith purchasers, and to enable the trade of property, the following means of retaining claimed property are provided by law: adverse possession, statutes of limitations (the discovery rule and the demand and refusal rule), and laches.

Adverse Possession, Statute of Limitations, Laches

A museum may obtain a new and paramount title to a potentially stolen object through the assertion of adverse possession. While typically used for real property (land), adverse possession may enable the current possessor to perfect title by showing possession of the property is "continuous, exclusive, hostile (i.e., clearly at odds with anyone else's assertion of title), open, and notorious"[3] for the period of time required by statute, as defined by state law. It can be difficult to prove each of these elements of fact—particularly that the item was held openly and notoriously—and the burden of proof lies with the possessor claiming title through adverse possession.

Adverse possession rules aim to provide owners a sufficiently long period of time to find and claim their stolen property; after this statutory period of time, the title is secured by the long-term possessor.[4] Until 1980, American courts applied adverse possession rules uniformly by commencing the prescription period at the time of the theft[5]; the theft itself was considered the cause of action. However, owners who searched diligently may not have been able to locate their stolen property or the thief, largely due to the movable nature of personal property. To mitigate this disadvantage to owners, courts modified the way that adverse possession rules are applied by changing the accrual period for the cause of action.

The length of the statute and the moment that the statute of limitations begins to run are determined by state law and are specific to the cause of action. For example, New York commences the limitation period after the item is discovered, a request is made for the return of the property, and the current possessor refuses to release the material. This distinction is referred to as the demand and refusal rule and greatly favors the original owners by lengthening the amount of time they may take action. A bona fide purchaser is perpetually vulnerable to the property being claimed by the original owner.[6] To retain his or her property, the bona fide purchaser only has recourse through the doctrine of laches, as described below. The demand and refusal rule is favorable to the prior owner and is important to many cultural property cases because New York is the center of the art market in the United States.

Most other states, however, balance the actions of the original owner and current possessor and provide for a "discovery rule," meaning the statute of limitations runs from the moment the claimant discovers—or, by performing reasonable due diligence research, should have discovered—the location of the stolen item. The rights of the current possessor and original owner are more balanced when the discovery rule is applied as "the victim's actions must be weighed in light of all the circumstances, including the actions of the possessor, in order to decide whether the victim has shown sufficient diligence to stop the running of the statue of limitations."[7]

The "doctrine of laches" is an equity-based approach that requires a full trial analyzing and weighing the actions of both parties. By applying laches, the possessor carries the burden to show the original owner "slept on his rights" by "negligently delaying taking action to the detriment of the defendant and that allowing that party to prevail would be unjust."[8] The discovery rule and laches rely on evidence of both parties' due diligence: the owner by reporting the theft and maintaining an ongoing search for their property, and the possessor by diligently researching the item's provenance and considering the possibility that the item may have been stolen. Courts have been unable to specify exactly what is required for due diligence; this has been decided on a case-by-case basis. However, openly sharing acquisition information and provenance, when possible, as well as thoroughly documenting the acquisition review process, including the myriad steps taken to ensure the museum has performed the necessary due diligence, should be considered mandatory procedural steps.

Absent state or local restrictions, archaeological resources on private land within the United States are most often controlled by the landowner where the object is located. Under the common law of finds, any material found embedded in or firmly affixed to the ground is granted to the owner of the land in which the object was embedded.[9] Determining the legal owner of property, particularly for archaeological material, is often a challenging undertaking. This topic is covered in more detail in Chapter 6.

These common-law principles apply so long as federal, state, or municipal statutes pose no contradiction. It should also be noted that the above rules are in line with the common-law legal system in place in the United States. Other countries may apply these defenses differently or not at all. This is particularly true of civil law jurisdictions, such as France, Switzerland, Germany, Japan, and Mexico, which follow a rule that gives a good faith purchaser good title after a fixed period of time, regardless of whether the item was stolen.[10] Civil law countries generally allow for a shorter statute of limitations during which the owner may take action.

There are particular types of property that are governed by rules beyond common-law principles; in fact, the legislation governing them may be contrary to the established common-law principles relating to private property. The following are nine examples of such exceptional material:

1. items obtained from burial sites
2. items obtained from archaeological sites on public lands
3. Native American and Native Hawaiian cultural property
4. foreign cultural material
5. treasure trove
6. items obtained from underwater archaeological sites or shipwrecks
7. human remains
8. Nazi-era material
9. items made from endangered species or fauna

Categories 5 through 9 above are not the focuses of this publication. However, resources for finding out more information on these property types are available in Appendix F. The specific rules governing the first four types of exceptional material are summarized below.

LEGAL CONSIDERATIONS FOR DOMESTIC CULTURAL PROPERTY

Table 2.1 summarizes the various legal means restricting the acquisition of cultural property that originated within the United States.

Introduction

The federal government does not exert control over archaeological materials found within the United States, with the exception of material

Table 2.1: Laws Governing the Acquisition of Domestic Cultural Property

Law	Citation and Year	Common Name
Antiquities Act of 1906	16 U.S.C. 431-433 (1906)	Antiquities Act
Archaeological Resources Protection Act	16 U.S.C. §§ 470aa-470mm (1979)	ARPA
Native American Graves Protection and Repatriation Act	Public Law 101-601, 25 U.S.C. §§ 3001-3013 (1990)	NAGPRA
National Stolen Property Act	18 U.S.C. § 2314-2315 (1948)	NSPA
Curation of federally owned and administered archaeological collections	36 C.F.R. pt 79.55 Fed. Reg. 37670 (1990)	36 CFR 79
State and local laws governing archaeological resources and burials as well as those covering crimes to property	Varies	State law
Property rights under common law	Varies	Common law or case law

from federally or tribally owned or administered land. Archaeological resources from federal lands are covered under several federal laws, primarily the Antiquities Act, the Archaeological Resources Protection Act (ARPA), and the Native American Graves Protection and Repatriation Act (NAGPRA). Tribal lands are covered under ARPA and NAGPRA. These three laws are summarized below. In addition, Sections 106 and 110 of the National Historic Preservation Act, the Archaeological and Historical Preservation Act, and the Reservoir Salvage Act impact archaeological material on public lands. These statutes, however, focus mainly on requiring federal agencies to protect and preserve archaeological and historical resources that may be impacted by federal projects.

Public lands constitute roughly one-third of the United States.[11] For the remaining two-thirds, archaeological resources on private land are most often controlled by the landowner where the object is located. Consequently, there are no federal laws that prohibit the unscientific excavation and removal of archaeological materials from private lands so long as the landowner consents. State and local laws may have some impact on the excavation, removal, or transfer of archaeological material but this impact is largely limited to specific circumstances, such as the excavation of burial sites and human remains. The sale of legally obtained archaeological materials is also not prohibited by federal law, although some states have regulations restricting sale of material from private properties.[12] Furthermore, acts violating state law and involving archaeological resources, as defined by ARPA, may enable the criminal penalties of ARPA if the item is involved in interstate commerce.[13] As discussed in Chapter 3, museums are advised to retain legal guidance in researching state laws to ensure their policies reflect local law. Resources for finding out more about state laws are provided in Chapter 6.

Antiquities Act of 1906

The Antiquities Act of 1906 was the first federal legislation designed to protect and preserve antiquities originating from within the United States. The act gave the president authority to select national monuments to be set aside for protection and required that the secretary of the federal department with jurisdiction over the protected land issue an antiquities permit prior to archaeological excavation. The law does not appear to transfer title of the excavated archaeological materials to the federal government. Section 3 of the act specifies that "the examinations, excavations, and gatherings are undertaken for the benefit of reputable museums, universities, colleges, or other recognized scientific or educational institutions, with a view to increasing the knowledge of such objects, and that the gatherings shall be made for permanent preservation in public museums."[14] Under this act, excavation, appropriation, damage or destruction of any prehistoric ruin or monument, or object of antiquity on federally controlled lands became punishable by law. Although deemed vague and difficult to enforce, the Antiquities Act was an important first step toward increased protection of the archaeological record on public lands. Archaeological resources excavated under a federally issued antiquities permit are subject to curation standards set forth in 36 CFR 79 regulations. The curatorial value of the material should be weighed against the burden of caring for the material in the manner specified in this regulation.

Archaeological Resources Protection Act (ARPA)

ARPA was enacted in 1979 to strengthen the Antiquities Act by clarifying the scope of protection and increasing penalty provisions. The archaeological investigation permit requirement established in the Antiquities Act is carried over in ARPA, but restrictions were added to cover tribally owned or controlled lands in addition to those under the purview of the federal government. ARPA asserts that ownership of archaeological resources removed from federally owned or controlled land is retained by the U.S. government. The Indian tribe owning or having jurisdiction over tribal land must consent to the excavation, transfer, and disposition of archaeological materials; these tribal entities retain ownership of material from these lands.

ARPA considerably broadens enforcement through more severe penalties including significantly larger fines and longer periods of incarceration for convicted violators.[15] It also provides detailed descriptions of prohibited activities and clear definitions of covered material; ARPA protects archaeological resources located on public lands and tribal lands by prohibiting their damage, removal, or unpermitted excavation and forbidding the sale, purchase, exchange, transport, receipt, or offer to sell, purchase, or exchange of these resources.[16] Furthermore, ARPA includes a catchall provision that makes it a crime to handle archaeological material in a way that violates state or local law, which may include activity on private property. Therefore, possessing or obtaining an item that one knows was taken without permission from private property in the United States would generally violate common-law principles of private property, as well as state criminal statutes, and, as we will see, this provision may also be applied to foreign property cases.

Clearly then, acquiring archaeological materials that are thought to be excavated from federal lands after 1906 and tribal lands after 1979 has legal implications. This material is also subject to government-mandated regulations for collections curation and care. Title 36, Part 79 of Chapter I of the Code of Federal Regulations (36 CFR 79), "Curation of Federally Owned and Administered Archaeological Collections," applies to collections that are excavated or removed under the authority of the Antiquities Act, the Reservoir Salvage Act, Section 110 of the National Historic Preservation Act, and the Archeological Resources Protection Act.[17] 36 CFR 79 applies to new and preexisting collections and to both material remains and associated records. Museums should balance the curatorial value of the cultural material against the burden of federal curation standards and enter into a depository agreement with the federal government if doing so is deemed beneficial.

Native American Graves Protection and Repatriation Act (NAGPRA)

Enacted in 1990, NAGPRA describes the rights of Native American lineal descendants, Indian tribes, and Native Hawaiian organizations regarding the repatriation, disposition, and treatment of cultural items, which include human remains, sacred objects, objects of cultural patrimony, and associated and unassociated funerary objects. These categories of cultural items and the definition for right of possession are defined in Chapter 6 and the Glossary in Appendix A. NAGPRA also reinforces many aspects of ARPA, as it protects Native American burial sites and other cultural resources within archaeological sites located on federal and tribal lands.

Importantly, NAGPRA includes criminal penalties for illegal trafficking in human remains or cultural items obtained in violation of the act. Knowingly selling, purchasing, using for profit, or transporting for sale or profit Native American human remains without the right of possession or any Native American cultural items obtained in violation of NAGPRA, meaning they were illegally removed from federal or Indian lands, will result in fines and imprisonment upon conviction.[18]

For over twenty years, federally funded museums have been required to inventory Native American human remains and associated funerary objects in their possession or control, identify their cultural and geographical affiliations, prepare summaries of information about the four categories of material covered by NAGPRA, consult with lineal descendants and Native American or Hawaiian groups, and repatriate objects and remains determined to be held without right of possession to groups showing cultural affiliation with the items in question.

As of March 15, 2010, with the passing of the NAGPRA Rule on the Disposition of Culturally Unidentifiable Human Remains,[19] museums must now also abide by procedures to address the disposition of human remains that are determined by museums to be Native American but lack affiliation with a present-day Indian tribe or Native Hawaiian organization or an identifiable earlier group. Museums must consult with Indian tribes and Native Hawaiian organizations whose tribal lands or aboriginal occupancy areas are in the area where the remains were removed, as they may request repatriation of the remains.

Also, under the 2007 NAGPRA Future Applicability Rule, if a museum receives new collections with items that fall into the NAGPRA cultural item categories or such items are discovered within the museum after inventory, or if a new tribal group becomes federally recognized, the museum is required to implement the summary, inventory, consultation, repatriation process for those items that meet the NAGPRA definition of cultural items.[20]

State and Municipal Laws

State statutes are the primary means of protecting archaeological materials on both publicly and privately owned lands. Laws governing archaeological resources differ greatly by state. Many states have archaeological protection laws similar to ARPA and NAGPRA, described above. These laws may include the following categories: "restrictions on the sale of antiquities, artifacts, and/or forgeries; ARPA-like resource management statutes that contain penalty provisions; burial protection and reinternment; and acquisition of real property and archaeological resources."[21] Often, restrictions are imposed primarily on state-owned properties and less frequently on private land listed on the State Register of Historic Places. Archaeological resources on private lands are covered by some state statutes. These laws may require "consent of the owner before anyone disturbs an archaeological site"[22] or "project review processes similar to Section 106 of the National Historic Preservation Act."[23] In addition, the protection of archaeological sites may be provided for by state statutes that have broader property applications such as theft, trespass, and vandalism.

Many states also have laws specifically intended to protect burials and cemeteries, and, as of 1994, approximately half had statutes specifically for the protection of unmarked human burials.[24] Generally, these laws include provisions for "consultation with, permission from, or supervision by, persons from an 'appropriate' present-day Indian tribe who may be affiliated with the persons whose graves are discovered."[25] Also, states generally have health and safety statutes outlining procedures for notifying authorities when marked or unmarked graves are found and prohibiting disturbance of such sites.

Municipal laws generally reinforce state statutes. However, archaeological excavations located on a locally designated historic property or district may be governed by town bylaws or under the authority of the municipal historical commission or city archaeologist. Historic properties may also have preservation restrictions or easements dictating the excavation and disposition of archaeological materials. These easements or preservation restrictions are agreements between landowners and local or state governments or other entities, which require future owners to abide by the terms set forth in the agreements.[26]

Furthermore, the National Stolen Property Act (NSPA) may be enforceable if the defendant knowingly transports a stolen item, or group of items, valued at more than $5,000. As mentioned, the criminal penalties outlined in ARPA may also be enforceable if this action involves archaeological resources and is in violation of state and local law. ARPA has been applied to unapproved removal of archaeological resources from private property as the actions were in violation of state laws of trespass and conversion.[27]

Legal Considerations for Foreign Cultural Property

The acquisition of certain types of cultural property originating from outside the United States is restricted by the regulations, legislation, conventions, and treaties listed in Table 2.2.

These rules, which impact the acquisition of cultural property originating outside the United States, can be divided broadly into two categories: those prohibiting import of certain materials, which, upon discovery, are subject to seizure and forfeiture, and those that regulate criminal behavior. While a broad generalization, this distinction is helpful in illustrating the legal landscape in which museums operate.

Table 2.2: Laws Governing the Acquisition of Foreign Cultural Material

Legal Mandate	Citation and Year	Common Name
Regulation of Importation of Pre-Columbian Monumental or Architectural Sculpture or Murals Act	19 USC §§ 2091-2095 Regulations: 19 CFR §§ 12.105-12.109 (1972)	Pre-Columbian Act
U.S. import restrictions	Varies	Customs sanctions or embargoes
Treaties/executive agreements between the United States of America and Ecuador, Guatemala, Mexico, and Peru	Varies	Treaties
UNESCO Convention on the Means of Prohibiting and Preventing the Illicit Import, Export, and Transfer of Ownership of Cultural Property	n/a 1970	UNESCO Convention
Convention on Cultural Property Implementation Act	Legislation: 19 USC §§ 2601-2613 (1983) Regulations: 19 CFR §§ 12.104-12.104i. (1982)	CPIA
National Stolen Property Act	18 U.S.C. § 2314-2315 (1948)	NSPA
Foreign cultural property laws	Varies	Varies
State Laws and Archaeological Resources Protection Act	ARPA 16 U.S.C. §§ 470ee(c) (1979) State laws vary	ARPA and state laws
Property rights under common law	Varies	Common law or case law

Executive and Legislative Rules Specifically Intended to Govern the Importation of Cultural Property

This section outlines those laws, conventions, treaties, and executive agreements that were specifically intended by the U.S. legislature to restrict the importation of specified classes of foreign cultural property identified as threatened by widespread looting. As these rules are essentially export laws, other customs restrictions are included here that result in embargoes on material originating from specific countries.

Regulation of Importation of Pre-Columbian Monumental or Architectural Sculpture or Murals

To address the destruction of archaeological resources in neighboring South and Central America, the United States entered into a series of treaties and executive agreements and enacted regulations intended to help stem the tide of archaeological site destruction and illicit trade and aid in the return of stolen property. The Regulation of Importation of Pre-Columbian Monumental or Architectural Sculpture or Murals Act was enacted in October 1972 and restricts importation of specific types of pre-Columbian artifacts originating from Bolivia, British Honduras (now Belize), Colombia, Costa Rica, Dominican Republic, Ecuador, El Salvador, Guatemala, Honduras, Mexico, Panama, Peru, or Venezuela into the United States. Any material originating from these countries and meeting the description of pre-Columbian monumental or architectural sculptures or murals requires certification from the country of origin that the material was legally exported; material lacking such evidence is subject to forfeiture.

Treaties of Cooperation with Mexico, Peru, Ecuador, and Guatemala

The Treaty of Cooperation between the United States of America and the United Mexican States Providing for the Recovery and Return of Stolen Archaeological, Historical, and Cultural Properties was signed in July 1970. This treaty stated that these countries intended to cooperate on the recovery and return of archaeological, historical, and cultural properties. These materials included items of outstanding importance to the national patrimony of both countries, including objects and artifacts of the pre-Columbian indigenous cultures, art objects and religious artifacts from the colonial period, and pre-1920 documents of historical importance taken from official archives.[28] This treaty does not appear to restrict importation; rather, its intent is to assist with the recovery and return of objects that fall into these categories. The treaty permits legitimate international commerce in art objects, consistent with both countries' laws and regulations.

Also, in the early 1980s, the United States also entered into agreements with Peru,[29] Ecuador,[30] and Guatemala[31] relating to the regulation of cultural property originating from these countries. Like the treaty with Mexico, these agreements do not restrict importation; rather, their intent is to assist with the recovery and return of stolen objects falling into specified categories of material that are the property of federal, state, or municipal governments or their instrumentalities.

U.S. Customs Restrictions

The Office of Foreign Assets Control of the U.S. Department of the Treasury administers and enforces a number of economic and trade sanctions. While enacted for the purposes of national security and foreign policy and not directly intended to address the specific issue of trade in foreign cultural property, these sanctions nonetheless impact the legality of material from certain countries. Sanctions currently cover cultural property originating from the Balkans, Belarus, Cuba, The Democratic Republic of the Congo, Côte d'Ivoire (Ivory Coast), Iran, Iraq, Liberia, Myanmar (Burma), North Korea, Somalia, Sudan, Syria, and Zimbabwe.[32]

UNESCO Convention on the Means of Prohibiting and Preventing the Illicit Import, Export, and Transfer of Ownership of Cultural Property

The United States signed the UNESCO Convention in 1970 and ratified it in 1972 with reservations and an understanding that any federal legislation implementing the agreement would need to be approved by the Senate and implemented by federal legislation. As one of the signatories to the UNESCO Convention, the United States agreed to work with other signatory nations, upon request, to prevent the import of, and trade in, archaeological and ethnographic materials and in stolen cultural collections. Not all aspects of the UNESCO Convention are legally binding in the United States. Implementing legislation was passed in 1983 through the Convention on Cultural Property Implementation Act.

The Convention on Cultural Property Implementation Act

The U.S. Convention on Cultural Property Implementation Act of 1983 (CPIA) is far narrower in scope than the UNESCO Convention, implementing only Articles 7(b) and 9 of the 1970 agreement. Therefore, not all articles of the UNESCO Convention are legally binding within the United States.

The CPIA makes a distinction between documented and undocumented objects. Under Section 308 of the CPIA, which implements Article 7(b) of the UNESCO Convention,

> no article of cultural property which was documented as being part of the inventory of a museum or religious or secular public monument or similar institution in any State Party which was stolen from such museum, monument, or institution after April 12, 1983, or after the date of entry into force of the UNESCO Convention for the State Party, whichever date is later, may be imported into the U.S.[33]

These documented items include objects that may be traced to official excavation sites in the country of origin.

There are different, more complicated procedures for dealing with undocumented archaeological and ethnological materials that are subject to looting and illicit trade. Materials in this category are not part of a museum or institution's official inventory; rather, these objects may be illegally excavated archaeological objects or illegally collected ethnographic objects from a country that ratified, accepted, or acceded to the

1970 UNESCO Convention. CPIA restricts importation of undocumented material only after the U.S. Cultural Property Advisory Committee reviews petitions for restrictions from countries party to the convention and makes recommendations to the president to enact bilateral agreements. After review, the president may choose to enact temporary restrictions, for no longer than five years, on certain types of objects. The countries requesting the import restriction enter into a bilateral agreement with the United States, which may be suspended or extended depending on the committee's findings. The president also has the authority to implement emergency actions, which immediately prohibit import of particular types of material under considerable threat of destruction. These procedures implement Article 9 of the UNESCO Convention.

As of November 16, 2010, bilateral or emergency agreements exist with thirteen countries, including Bolivia, Cambodia, China, Columbia, Cyprus, El Salvador, Guatemala, Honduras, Iraq, Italy, Mali, Nicaragua, and Peru. The 1997 agreement with Canada expired in 2002.[34]

CPIA did not put into practice Article 7(a) of the UNESCO Convention, which sought to "prevent museums and similar institutions within their territories from acquiring cultural property originating in another State Party which has been illegally exported after entry into force of this Convention, in the States concerned" and "[w]henever possible, to inform a State of origin Party to this Convention if an offer of such cultural property illegally removed from that State after the entry into force of this Convention in both States."[35] Hence, CPIA does not restrict the collecting practices of U.S. museums beyond the restriction of acquiring stolen documented material and undocumented material specifically covered by agreements and emergency actions. Congress believed that museums would implement collecting policies that voluntarily adopted the standards expressed in CPIA and the UNESCO Convention.

CPIA, as well as the other legal means described above, are intended to prohibit or regulate the importation of specific types of cultural property and do not broadly restrict the exchange of cultural property. However, legal precedents indicate that the cultural property laws of foreign nations clearly claiming ownership of cultural property will be upheld in U.S. courts and the criminal penalties outlined in NSPA or ARPA may be enforceable.

U.S. Judicial Decisions and the Recognition of Foreign Government Ownership of Cultural Property

The U.S. legal system does not view the unauthorized export or import of another country's cultural property a violation of U.S. law.[36] Indeed, doing so is "arguably contrary to the settled principle of private international law that one nation will not enforce the criminal laws of another."[37] National legislation is generally considered binding only within that nation's own territory, lacking jurisdiction outside of state borders. However, several legal precedents have enforced cultural property laws that specifically claim ownership of this material. While some foreign cultural property laws merely prohibit export of certain types of property, others are comprehensive in their scope of coverage, frequently claiming ownership of anything within the ground within their national boundaries, both documented and yet to be discovered. It has become increasingly important for museum professionals to have a thorough understanding of the laws governing the acquisition of cultural property, including U.S. legislation and those in foreign countries, and how these laws may impact collecting.

National Stolen Property Act and Foreign Cultural Property Laws

The U.S. Court of Appeals in the Second,[38] Fifth,[39] and Ninth[40] Circuits have recognized government ownership of cultural property as asserted in laws of foreign nations, thereby subjecting individuals who knowingly imported property in violation of these laws to criminal penalties under NSPA.

NSPA makes it a crime, punishable by either a fine or imprisonment, to knowingly possess a stolen item worth more than $5,000 and transport it across state lines. Conscious avoidance—purposefully remaining ignorant of the law in order to avoid consequences—is not considered an acceptable defense.[41] The only requirement of NSPA is knowledge that the goods were stolen, which is largely determined by the defendant's actions.

During the 1970s, the decade when the U.S. Congress was debating how to implement the UNESCO Convention, NSPA was successfully applied in two cases regarding imported antiquities. The first criminal prosecution, *U.S. v. Hollinshead*,[42] involved a pre-Columbian stela that had been illicitly removed from an archaeological site documented by Ian Graham, a noted Mayan archaeologist. The defendants knew their conduct was illegal based on the Guatemalan law asserting national ownership, thus supporting the conviction under NSPA. In Hollinshead, the stolen object was clearly identifiable and previously documented, which was not the case in subsequent legal cases.

In 1977, *U.S. v. McClain*[43] set the precedent for U.S. courts recognizing other countries' cultural patrimony laws as determining ownership of undocumented antiquities. In McClain, a criminal case, defendants were convicted of conspiring to transport stolen artifacts from Mexico in violation of a Mexican law asserting ownership, and hence, in violation of NSPA. Both appeals upheld the conviction under NSPA because the court agreed to fully recognize the 1972 Mexican law, which was written with sufficient clarity to claim state ownership of all pre-Columbian antiquities.[44]

NSPA was applied unsuccessfully in *Peru v. Johnson*,[45] a 1989 case that was thought to weaken the McClain doctrine. Johnson brought to light several important considerations for those dealing in foreign cultural property. The Court established that the source country's cultural patrimony law must be sufficiently clear to U.S. citizens and fully enforced within the borders of that country. Further, there must be evidence that the object was exported after the effective date of the cultural property law and that the object can be clearly shown to have originated in that particular country. The case also made an important distinction between an export law and an ownership law. The Court determined that Peru's patrimony laws did not clearly vest ownership of undocumented antiquities with the country; rather, they were viewed as export controls, which are not enforced by U.S. courts.[46]

The McClain doctrine was not applied successfully for over twenty-five years to prosecute cultural property cases. During this period, however, the U.S. courts did uphold another country's ownership rights to cultural property on other grounds. In 1997, the U.S. courts again upheld a foreign country's ownership law when ruling on *U.S. v. An Antique Platter of Gold*,[47] which is also referred to as the Steinhardt case. This case involved the customs seizure of an Italian antiquity purchased by a wealthy New York collector. The seizure was requested by the government of Italy, which claimed that the object was stolen, as defined by a 1939 Italian law. While the trial court upheld the foreign statute vesting ownership of the item in Italy, bringing the case under NSPA, the appellate court upheld the forfeiture based on falsified customs declarations rather than the transport of stolen property.[48]

However, the McClain doctrine was successfully applied in the 2002 *U.S. v. Schultz*[49] case, which resulted in the conviction of Frederick Schultz, a prominent dealer in ancient art, for conspiring to deal in antiquities stolen from Egypt. The Court determined that a 1983 Egyptian law clearly vested ownership of all antiquities discovered after that date in Egypt; any antiquities excavated after 1983 and removed without permission were stolen property under Egyptian law.[50] The law was determined to be sufficiently clear, familiar to those in the art world, enforced fully within Egypt, and went beyond restricting export by clearly vesting ownership in the government of Egypt. Schultz's actions were ruled to be clearly fraudulent in nature, an indication of scienter—acting to knowingly deceive, manipulate, or defraud.[51]

As with NSPA, ARPA is generally enforced when the item is involved in interstate commerce, allowing for involvement of the federal government. However, NSPA's scienter requirement is circumvented in the application of

ARPA. Under NSPA, the federal government needs to prove the defendant knew the object in question was stolen. Under ARPA, however, the government is not required to prove the defendant knew property is stolen, only that the defendant knowingly received archaeological resources that have been obtained or removed in violation of state law.[52]

The Relationship between Archaeological Resources Protection Act, State Laws, and Foreign Cultural Property Laws

Section 470ee(c) of ARPA states that:

> No person may sell, purchase, exchange, transport, receive, or offer to sell, purchase, or exchange, in interstate or foreign commerce, any archaeological resource excavated, removed, sold, purchased, exchanged, transported, or received in violation of any provision, rule, regulation, ordinance, or permit in effect under State or local law.[53]

Therefore, actions that violate state laws and involve archaeological resources as defined by ARPA may be prosecuted under ARPA, a federal criminal law. Also, in addition to the reduced burden of proof required for ARPA compared to NSPA, the valuation requirement is significantly less at only $500, compared to $5,000.

There have been three instances where ARPA was applied to foreign property,[54] the most recent of which involved the January 2008 raids of four California museums for evidence pertaining to illicit archaeological materials. Importantly, the affidavits in the California case seem to lay "a foundation for the possible indictment of museum staffers allegedly complicit in the looting schemes—which would be a first under American law."[55]

The statutory overview provided in the affidavits reference two California state laws. One of the laws made it a criminal act to receive property stolen in another country and bring it into California knowing the property was stolen.[56] The other state law asserts that anyone involved in the commission of a crime, who has advised and encouraged its commission or aided and abetted in its commission, has violated state law.[57]

The investigations concerned archaeological resources originating from Thailand, China, Burma, and from federal and tribal lands in New Mexico. Artifacts from Cambodia, Guatemala, and El Salvador were also mentioned in additional search warrants released by federal authorities.[58] The federal agents argue that all of these places of origin, with the exception of Burma, are covered by ARPA as the countries of origin all have broad cultural property legislation declaring government ownership of all antiquities, whether these items are known or as yet discovered. Material from Burma, also known as Myanmar, is restricted from importation per Executive Order No. 13047 and by the Burmese Freedom and Democracy Act of 2003. The affidavits effectively lay out the following argument: if the country of origin has a cultural property law, and a U.S. state makes knowingly importing material that is taken in violation of a foreign ownership law a crime, then federal ARPA legislation would also be violated if the material involved could be defined as archaeological resources or human remains as defined by ARPA. While the application of ARPA to the material originating from tribal and federal lands in New Mexico is expected, its use in criminalizing the act of importing foreign property in violation of foreign law has been argued by some to be beyond the intended scope of the law.[59]

During the course of the California investigation, an undercover agent from the National Park Service acquired illegally exported items from a wholesale dealer and smuggler, Robert Olson, and gallery owner Jonathan Markell. These items were subsequently donated to local museums at inflated prices, enabling the undercover agent to take fraudulent tax deductions. The homes and businesses of Olson and Markell, as well as four California museums, were raided in January 2008 as part of this investigation. The affidavits state that the museums have been involved in receiving stolen property, import violations, and tax fraud.

What makes the current U.S. federal investigation particularly significant—and alarming for those working with antiquities collections—is that the inquiry was not initiated abroad; rather, the investigation was instigated by federal agencies.[60] In contrast, the McClain and Schultz cases, as well as the various negotiated agreements between museums and foreign countries, have resulted from foreign governments asserting their ownership of items illegally taken from their country.

As mentioned, some feel that the application of NSPA and ARPA in criminalizing trade in cultural property has relegated the CPIA to importation restriction status, negating the legislative intent of the act.[61] Critics have also asserted that the enforcement of foreign country patrimony laws in U.S. courts is contrary to U.S. and international legal rules of state sovereignty.[62] However, these legal decisions are now set as precedent in case law and will likely be influential in findings of similar cases. These convictions have "shifted the burden to prove an object's good standing onto museums and collectors"[63] and required a reconsideration of the longstanding "don't ask, don't tell"[64] policy, which had traditionally been utilized by many museums when negotiating a purchase from a dealer or acceptance of a donation. Therefore, museums must be vigilant in their efforts to abide by state laws as well as foreign cultural patrimony laws.

As the cases discussed above show, those convicted under NSPA were aware of the illegal nature of their actions as their behavior was intentionally fraudulent in nature, and those convicted under ARPA knew that the items were obtained in violation of state law. Museums may acquire cultural material after performing the due diligence research necessary to ensure that doing so will not violate the law, thereby acting in good faith. The procedural guidelines in the following chapters describe steps for working within the legal landscape summarized above. Before these procedures can be implemented, however, a museum must clearly define its specific policy to guide in the acquisition of cultural material. The next chapter will assist a museum craft such a policy.

Chapter 3

Crafting an Acquisition Policy for Antiquated Cultural Property and Archaeological Material

The acquisition of archaeological material and antiquated cultural property poses significant risks in terms of public appearance, financial and staff time investments, and legal liability. Furthermore, each acquisition comes at the cost of permanent care and stewardship. The museum must ensure that the limited financial, space, and staff resources are appropriately utilized and balanced by the benefit that an acquisition may offer. Museum staff must be able to refer to carefully considered and articulated instructions that have been approved by the museum's governing board and legal counsel, and incorporate the legal rules governing acquisitions in their state, as well as the institutional and ethical considerations unique to their museum. This chapter guides museums through the process of crafting a policy to govern the acquisition of antiquated cultural property and archaeological material, which will work within the legal landscape described in Chapter 2.

The policy development procedures outlined in this chapter were significantly influenced by my experience of proposing a similar draft policy for the Harvard University Peabody Museum of Archaeology and Ethnology (PMAE) in 2006. Under the direction of Dr. Genevieve Fisher, registrar, and Dr. Patricia Capone, associate curator, draft versions of the museum's basic criteria, ethical considerations, and institutional considerations for acquisitions were developed. The guidelines provided below were not specifically developed for PMAE; instead, they represent a more generalized version that reflect common principles found in many other museums' policies as well as the overarching and current legal principles governing the acquisition of antiquated cultural property and archaeological material. The ethical and institutional considerations provided may be thought of as best practices that can be adopted or modified by other institutions. The basic criteria for acquisition discussed may also be customized for a particular institution, as discussed below.

The recommended steps for crafting a policy outlined in Table 3.1 merges the course of action proposed for the PMAE when developing its policy with best practices for collections management policy development provided by John Simmons in *Things Great and Small: Collections Management Policies*.[1]

A policy specifically intended to guide staff in the acquisition of cultural property and archaeological material is only one part of a museum's collections management policy, which is broader in scope and typically covers care of collections, records and inventories, deaccesssioning, access, loans, and a myriad of other topics. Due to the complexity and number of issues that impact an institution's specific approach to acquisition of antiquated cultural property and archaeological material, in this chapter I walk museum staff through the process of considering the various decisions one must make in crafting a policy specific to this topic and the possible implications of these decisions (see Table 3.1).

This chapter does not review in detail all steps listed in Table 3.1 but focuses on steps 6–9, development of the components of the museum's acquisition policy for antiquated cultural property and archaeological material. Recommendations for developing procedures, requesting and reviewing provenance and provenience information from vendor/donors, and reviewing the legality and ethicality of the acquisition and the completeness of title will be discussed in subsequent chapters.

Philosophical Viewpoints and Organizational Affiliations Influencing Museum Policies and Practices

The particular professional organization(s) with which a museum affiliates may influence collecting policies and practices. The American Association of Museums (AAM),[2] the Association of Art Museum Directors (AAMD),[3] the Archaeological Institute of America (AIA),[4] and the International Council of Museums (ICOM)[5] are the primary professional organizations that offer museums guidance, in the form of standards, reports, recommendations, and codes of ethics, regarding the acquisition of foreign cultural material. This section summarizes the primary distinguishing characteristics of these organizations' policies but it does not describe all subtle distinctions, so museums should review these policies in full.

AIA and ICOM offer their guidance in the form of codes of ethics, which outline minimum standards for practice that member museums are expected to abide by. Museums abiding by these codes of ethics accept that due diligence research should uncover the full history of a potential

Table 3.1: Recommended Steps for Crafting a Policy, and Implementing a Procedure, to Guide the Acquisition of Antiquated Cultural Property and Archaeological Material

Step 1	Museum director should educate the governing authority on the importance of an acquisitions policy and procedure (and possibly illustrate the risk of not having one by referring examples of bad publicity or returned items).
Step 2	Museum director and governing authority review the museum's ethics and mission statements and revise as needed.
Step 3	Select members for the writing committee by choosing representatives from different areas of responsibility (i.e., curators, registrar, administration, collections, governing board, education, public relations, etc.).
Step 4	Draft a detailed description of the museum's existing collections and work with curatorial departments to define specific collection-related goals.
Step 5	Write a policy development statement that outlines the goals of the policy and the principles that will serve to guide in the policy developing process. Define common vocabulary to facilitate communication.
Step 6	Review the guidelines, standards, or recommendations provided by the professional organizations with which your institution allies.
Step 7	Retain legal counsel to analyze state laws, as outlined below.
Step 8	Draft the basic criteria for acquisitions, both for domestic and foreign cultural property. Certain basic criteria may be customized based on the requirements of state law as well as the museum's institutional and ethical considerations.
Step 9	Draft ethical and institutional considerations to be reviewed in conjunction with the basic criteria for acquisitions.
Step 10	Draft procedures for requesting provenance and provenience information from vendors/donors and determine acceptable forms of documentation. Create acquisition questionnaire and guidelines.
Step 11	Draft specific procedures for reviewing the legality, institutional appropriateness, and ethicality of an acquisition.
Step 12	Solicit feedback from staff; revise as needed.
Step 13	Solicit feedback on basic criteria for acquisition and procedural review from legal counsel; revise as needed.
Step 14	Present to the museum's governing authority; revise as needed. Acquire approval.
Step 15	Educate staff on policies and procedures and then implement.
Step 16	Publish policy online.
Step 17	Provide for periodic review and revision of all documents.

acquisition from its initial creation or excavation to the present and that the item must have resulted from an authorized, scientific excavation, disclosed to and approved by the government or property owner. These standards apply to both domestic and foreign archaeological material.

Further, all acquisitions must abide by all legal rules, both domestic and foreign. This includes ensuring a foreign property was exported legally, regardless of the date of exportation.

During the summer of 2008, both AAM and AAMD considerably strengthened their organizations' recommendations through the *Report of the AAMD Task Force on the Acquisition of Archaeological Materials and Ancient Art* and AAM's *Standards Regarding Archaeological Material and Ancient Art.* Both organizations adopted the date of the UNESCO Convention for the Protection of Cultural Property, November 17, 1970, after which date museums are expected to apply more rigorous standards before acquiring foreign cultural property. ICOM, AIA, and AAM either recommend or require that museums consider the laws of the country of modern discovery, and in some cases the laws of any intermediate countries, to ensure that items that have a pre-1970 provenance were not transported in violation of a foreign law that prohibited exportation at the time the item left the country. In contrast, AAMD's policy states that adherence to foreign export laws applies only after the 1970 cutoff date, which implies that acquiring an object that was exported in violation of foreign law prior to 1970 is generally acceptable.

Both AAM and AAMD's 2008 policies allow for the acquisition of foreign property that, after extensive research, has "substantial but not full documentation."[6] Lacking complete documentation, AAMD asserts that "an informed judgment" can be made as to whether an item meets its guidelines and can therefore be acquired. AAMD further instructs members to consider "the cumulative facts and circumstances resulting from provenance research, including, but not limited to, the independent exhibition and publication of the work, the length of time it has been on public display and its recent ownership history."[7] It appears that deference to publication and exhibition history provides additional flexibility regarding the acquisition of items lacking conclusive evidence the item was out of its country of origin by 1970 or had been legally exported after this date, as they may be able to point to this as evidence that due notice had previously been given to the original owner of the work. So long as the museum's acquisition is consistent with the statement of principles included in the AAMD report, is transparent about the provenance information and other facts relating to the decision-making process, and shares this information on the AAMD Registry of New Acquisitions of Archaeological Material and Works of Ancient Act,[8] museums may make an informed judgment to acquire the object. AAM similarly provides for flexibility for items lacking full documentation and requests museums be "transparent about why this is an appropriate decision in alignment with the institution's collections policy and applicable ethical codes."[9]

It should be noted that recommendations offered by AAM and AAMD are guidelines and recommendations, not mandated policy. One could adopt the policies outright, look at these policies as a minimum threshold to be further strengthened, or modify these policies to allow for increased flexibility. The onus is on the museum to have a sufficient understanding of the legal regulations and to understand the risks associated with its decisions.

Furthermore, in an effort to show increased transparency regarding the underlying decision-making process governing acquisitions, it is now a commonly held professional expectation that museums share their acquisition policies online.

Drafting Basic Criteria for Acquisition

To address the unique needs and philosophy of its institution as well as the framework mandated by professional standards and the law, a museum should determine the basic criteria necessary for an object to be considered for acquisition. Potential acquisitions fall into two distinct categories: items originating within the United States and those originating outside of the United States. It is necessary to develop separate legal criteria for both categories, as the legal rules governing U.S. and international acquisitions differ, although common-law principles and adherence to the National Stolen Property Act and state laws apply universally.

A number of the basic criteria for acquisition should remain essentially the same for all museums, perhaps varying in the type of documentation or degree of proof required, as they are governed by specific legal restrictions, and are fundamentally nonnegotiable. This is particularly true for domestic material originating from public or tribal lands, certain types of Native American, Alaskan and Hawaiian cultural material, categories of imported pre-Columbian material, and items restricted by emergency and bilateral agreements under CPIA.

As discussed, professional organizations and museums have applied specific cutoff dates or other criteria to address other legal rules governing the exchange of foreign property. This is particularly true of material originating from foreign countries that do not have a specific agreement with the United States restricting importation but it can also be applied to domestic material lacking conclusive provenance or provenience.

There is general consensus that museums must comply with all applicable local, state, and federal U.S. laws, including treaties and international conventions of which the United States is a party. To ensure basic criteria are grounded in all applicable law, it is therefore strongly advised that museums retain legal counsel to aid in policy development and/or review. Museums should additionally seek legal guidance on the following legal rules within the museum's state:

1. What state laws impact the excavation and disposition of archaeological materials found in the state, on both private and state lands?
2. Is there a law in the museum's state that makes it a crime to receive property stolen in another country and bring it into the state knowing the property was stolen, such as California Penal Code 497? (Found in California General Laws under Crimes to Property; Larceny.)
3. What is the statute of limitations for theft and possession of stolen goods in the state, and what commences and halts the running of that statute of limitations?

The museum should also be familiar with the various crimes to property statutes in the state that apply to all types of property. These statutes cover larceny, theft, conversion, purchase, transport or possession of stolen goods, and trespass. These laws may prohibit possession of items defined as stolen under state statutes, and, if the item was transported across state lines, the federal criminal penalties outlined in ARPA and NSPA may enforceable. Information regarding state laws provided by legal counsel should be incorporated into the basic criteria for acquisition to ensure the museum's policy adheres to the laws of their particular state, and a summary of the above laws should be provided to the museum for reference.

The process of drafting basic criteria for acquisition requires extensive deliberation and is largely one of risk assessment and management. Museums must balance the benefits of acquiring the property with the implications of future claims and/or criminal liability, the unintended impact that the acquisition may have on the continued destruction of archaeological context and on the public's perception of the museum, as well as the various costs associated with its perpetual care. The goal should be to provide museum staff with a sufficiently detailed set of guidelines to ensure they act in accordance to the institution's chosen policy.

The questions in Table 3.2 include considerations a museum should address when drafting their customized basic criteria. These considerations are not mutually exclusive. For each customized criterion, museums may specify differing degrees of documentation, or provide for exceptions to the rule if they meet specific requirements. The considerations and examples provided below do not cover all possible permutations but include many of the distinctions identified during a review of over thirty museum acquisition policies as well as the professional organization recommendations.

Table 3.2: Primary Questions to Consider when Drafting Customized Basic Criteria for Acquisition

Consideration	Examples
Does the museum require documented provenance dating to a specific cutoff date for certain types of acquisitions? If so, specifically for what property types and origins, and what must the date ensure?	For foreign items: • 1970 (UNESCO), 1983 (CPIA), or other • Other? – in the United States by (an established date) – outside country of origin or intermediate country by (an established date) – legally obtained, exported, and/or imported by (an established date) For domestic items lacking evidence of transfer of title: • 1978 (predate ARPA) – in private collection by (an established date) • Other – predate applicable state statutes
Are there special criteria necessary for acquisition?	General: – scientific excavation – known provenience – full provenance from discovery to present For U.S. material: – permission of landowner – consultation with tribal group For foreign material: – adherence to country of origin's law with effective date prior to museum's cutoff date – determination if foreign law is an ownership or export law – country of origin party to the UNESCO Convention
Are any exceptions made to above; if so, for what specifically?	• Minor objects valued at less than $5,000 (not subject to NSPA) • Fragments of ceramic pieces already in collection and not in violation of state law • For U.S. material, material with unknown provenience but recorded provenance back to a particular date (for example, pre-ARPA 1978), and not in violation of state law • Objects originating from within museum's state if a depository agreement can be arranged officially with the state • For the purpose of offering a "safe harbor" to prevent random disposal that would distort the archaeological record, preserve significant archaeological information, and/or promote public education about the value of archaeological investigations *in situ*

Continued

Table 3.2: *continued*

Consideration	Examples
What degree of assurance is required? Note: Museums should define what would constitute such assurance. See questions regarding documentation.	• Irrefutable proof or documented evidence • Reasonable assurance under the circumstance • No indication of violation • Professional judgment
What types of documentation are required to establish said degree of assurance? (Additional documentation is listed in Chapter 5.)	• Account of donor • Warranty/indemnity from vendor/donor • Deed of gift • Signed affidavit • Excavation permits and/or field notes • Export permits and/or import permits • Authentication of permits for items valued over specific amount • Exhibition or publication history (published or exhibited by specified date, length or venue of exhibition, distribution of publication) • Art registry search for works valued over specified amount
Are there other restrictions, exceptions, or considerations?	• Contact tribal government, or country of origin and wait specified period of time prior to acquiring • Accept as donation but do not purchase archaeological material • Accept item on loan and defer acquisition until certain period after the item is exhibited/published • Consult with legal counsel regarding completeness of title or running of statutes of limitations
How will transparency regarding the acquisition be achieved?	• Contact tribal government, state archaeologist, or country of origin • Post acquisition, including photos, provenance information, and reason for exception on museum's website, or in AAMD database (if AAMD member museum)

The resulting criteria may reflect ethical factors such as the goal of discouraging unscientific excavations of archaeological materials, recognition of the value of making a work of art publicly accessible, prevention of random disposal that would distort the archaeological record, preservation of significant archaeological information, and promotion of public education about the value of archaeological investigations *in situ*. While these principles are integral to establishing the basic criteria for acquisition, it is advisable for the museum to craft separate ethical and institutional considerations. These additional issues can either be reviewed in concert with the basic criteria or after determination of the appropriateness of the acquisition based on the established basic criteria.

Tables 3.3 and 3.4 provide examples of the basic criteria for acquisition for domestic and foreign objects, respectively. These rules are in addition to ensuring that the donor or vendor is authorized to transfer complete title and affirming the acquisition poses no conflict with state law. Specific information on what type of material is covered by each basic criterion, as well as the necessary documentation to prove compliance, is discussed in subsequent chapters.

November 17, 1970, the date of the UNESCO Convention on the Means of Prohibiting and Preventing the Illicit Import, Export and Transfer of Ownership of Cultural Property, is incorporated into the basic criteria for acquisition of foreign cultural material provided for example in Table 3.4. Although this date is a commonly adopted threshold that distinguishes the level of scrutiny and documentation required, adherence to this date is fundamentally an ethical distinction, not a legal one. As discussed, AAMD's policy seems to indicate that acquiring any item that can be shown to have been in the United States prior to November 17, 1970 is acceptable, regardless of any laws in the originating or intermediate country at the time of exportation. While this is a relatively common distinction cited by museums, it should be noted that it poses a degree of risk because doing so does not consider the legality of items transferred prior to this date.

Table 3.3: Examples of Basic Criteria for Acquisition of Domestic Cultural Material

1.	Require permits and other documentation for archaeological resources or cultural items originating from federally owned or controlled lands after 1905.
2.	Require permits and other documentation for archaeological resource or cultural items originating from tribally owned or controlled lands after 1978.
3.	Have reasonable assurance the object was not illegally excavated from lands controlled by any state or municipal statutes (particularly those relating to burial sites or restricting the sale, transport, or possession of archaeological material) after the effective date of applicable statutes.
4.	Have reasonable assurance that any cultural items as defined by NAGPRA (human remains, associated or unassociated funerary objects, sacred objects, or objects of cultural patrimony) are being transferred with clear right of possession.
5.	Require evidence the owner of the private property where the archaeological material originated permitted the excavation, removal, and transfer of the object and renounced further claims to the object, with possible exceptions as defined by the museum.

Table 3.4: Examples of Basic Criteria for Acquisition of Foreign Cultural Material

1.	Require evidence the object is not covered under the regulation of importation of pre-Columbian monumental or architectural sculpture or murals.
2.	Require evidence that the object is not designated as restricted under the Convention on Cultural Property Implementation Act.
3.	Have reasonable assurance the object was not reported stolen by a foreign country.
4.	Have reasonable assurance the item was not subject to U.S. customs import restrictions or sanctions.
5.	Require evidence the object was not exported after November 17, 1970 in violation of export or ownership laws of the country of origin and/or the country where it was last legally owned.
6.	Have reasonable assurance the item was not exported before November 17, 1970 in violation of foreign law, with possible exceptions as defined by museum.
7.	Require evidence the object was legally imported into the United States after November 17, 1970 or have reasonable assurance the item was legally imported prior to this date, with possible exceptions as defined by museum.

Exceptions, Under-Documentation, and Other Grey Areas

As a rule, staff must assume that if an object lacks sufficient provenance or provenience documentation to prove compliance with the established basic criteria for acquisition then it is not acquirable. Museums may choose to incorporate specific conditions that could allow for the acquisition of under-documented objects in certain situations, but these exceptions should be fully vetted and approved by the museum's governing authority and legal counsel. The decision to apply these exceptions is essentially an issue of ethics and risk assessment. A valuable lens is the appearance of the acquisition, in addition to the likelihood and appearance of a subsequent claim for return of the item, to descendant communities, the media, and the general public. Exceptions to the example basic criteria for acquisition described as Requiring Evidence in Tables 3.3 and 3.4 should be avoided.

While defining and incorporating exceptions to the basic criteria for acquisition is by no means a requirement for museums that wish to have a strict policy or are motivated by other philosophical considerations, it is highly recommended for those who wish to pursue acquisitions that lack the degree of documentation desirable today. This lack of documentation does not always indicate that an object is illicit or that acquiring it will have any negative implications on present-day archaeological site destruction. It is possible that the item was transferred within a family or held by an individual for a significant period of time, but with little accompanying documentation, a common situation for older, family-held collections. Museums should not accept the word of the donor or vendor as fact without supporting documentation, but they may wish to define the specific parameters that would allow for the acquisition of items lacking conclusive documentation. Lacking these specific parameters, a museum may find it easy to justify acquisition of increasingly ethically and legally questionable items and by doing so will negate the usefulness and protection of a clearly defined acquisition policy.

Exceptions to the rule should be rare and carefully considered, and the decision-making process should be well documented and shared transparently. The museum should not consider acquiring an object that would, in any actual or perceived way, support the clandestine excavation of archaeological materials and the illegal import of such. As with all acquisitions, the museum's basic criteria for acquisition, ethical and institutional considerations, and mission should guide the decision-making process.

The categorizations of "minor objects" and "older collections," and the distinction between "export laws" and "ownership laws" for foreign material, as discussed below, are examples of possible exceptions a museum may chose to apply to their basic criteria for acquisition. Note that these illustrations are offered for the purposes of discussion, but are not intended as recommendations for practice for any specific institution. Importantly, the onus is on the museum to understand the legal, ethical, and public relations implications of these distinctions and devise an appropriate policy for its institution.

The category "older collection" defines a domestic item of antiquity that has documented provenance dating back to at least 1978. The 1978 cutoff date is somewhat arbitrary, intended only to predate material subject to ARPA.[10] This provision takes into account that a great deal of archaeological material lacks detailed provenience information, but if proof of ownership since 1978 is available, the acquisition would not appear to promote unscientific excavation.

A "minor item" is an object (or group of objects) valued at $5,000 or less that has significant but not complete documentation dating to the museum's established cutoff date. This term applies to material originating from within and outside of the United States. The $5,000 value is based on the definition of objects covered under the NSPA, but this distinction is not made under ARPA and may only be considered so long as state law does not appear to prohibit the sale, transport,

Continued

Exceptions, Under-Documentation, and Other Grey Areas *(continued)*

purchase, or possession of the item under consideration. This distinction may be more appropriate for items with provenance information dating back to 1978, pre-ARPA, although the action may still be in violation of state property laws. The museum should recognize that these minor items may have originated from the same environment as other, more valuable items, "historically significant sites with associated archaeological remains,"[11] and in aggregate, the acquisition of these items could contribute to illicit trade and site destruction.

For foreign material, a museum may wish to determine if a foreign property law is an "export law," which prohibits export of certain types of material, or an "ownership law," which clearly deeds ownership of this material to the government. It is recommended that this determination be made with the assistance of legal counsel. This distinction has been incorporated into the basic criteria for foreign material only for material exported before the museum's cutoff date, but after the effective date of a foreign law clearly deeding ownership.

These categories are not recommendations; they are examples of how a museum may define specific parameters to allow for additional flexibility assuming previously specified and accepted criteria are met. All of these exceptions must be accompanied by a credible account of provenance from a trustworthy donor. If, as a result of due diligence, the museum finds the item to be clear of illegal or questionable nature, including objects appearing "freshly excavated, from a 'hot' area, or a 'hot' category of item,"[12] then the museum could decide to accept the object upon receipt of a signed or notarized warrant of title or affidavit. This document should warrant the item's provenance and state that the museum will not be held responsible for any expenses incurred by ownership claims made by a foreign country, tribal group, or other party.

Drafting Institutional and Ethical Considerations

While the legality of the acquisition must be the museum's first priority, the process of determining the suitability of an acquisition is governed by more than legislation, policies, and professional standards. Institutional and ethical factors must also be taken into consideration, and these factors generally apply to acquisitions from all geographic areas. As such, having updated and clearly articulated mission and ethics statements are extremely important preliminary steps in the process of drafting the basic criteria governing the acquisition of archaeological material and antiquated cultural property. These documents serve as touchstones during policy development, as well as during the procedural review of an acquisition. In addition, museums should formulate institutional and ethical considerations that address additional issues specifically concerning cultural property acquisitions. When reviewed in concert with the legality of the acquisition, these additional considerations (or criteria, if you wish to require adherence to such statements), will provide additional guidance to staff tasked with acquiring artifacts on behalf of the institution.

Sample institutional and ethical considerations are provided in Tables 3.5 and 3.6, respectively. Similarly worded statements are frequently incorporated into museum policies. While these criteria are rather ubiquitous in museum policies, this does not diminish their importance.

In drafting the museum's policy regarding the acquisition of archaeological material and antiquated cultural property, one should remember the basic criteria, as well as the institutional and ethical considerations are intended to provide adequate guidance for museum staff acting on behalf of the institution. All statements should be worded with sufficient clarity to ensure that material considered for acquisition is appropriate for that institution, and procedures should be established and documented to ensure compliance with the intended policy. These documents are more than mere words; they are the embodiment of a museum's philosophy and will serve as a touchstone for all deliberations regarding acquisitions.

Table 3.5: Sample Institutional Considerations for Acquisitions

1.	The object supports the museum's mission and public trust responsibilities.
2.	The object is valuable for the purposes of education, research, and other programmatic purposes.
3.	The object warrants the use of the museum's financial, personnel, and physical resources to ensure its proper storage, protection, care, documentation, and accessibility, in keeping with professionally accepted standards.
4.	The object's title is transferred free and clear, without restrictions.
5.	The object poses no or negligible risk to the safety of museum staff, visitors, or other objects within the collection; or, if the condition of object is compromised, its treatment and storage needs are balanced by its curatorial value.
6.	The object meets a specific need, or fills a specific gap in the existing collection, and this need can be articulated as a collecting priority by the curatorial staff.

Table 3.6: Sample Ethical Considerations for Acquisitions

1. The acquisition is consistent with the museum's desire to promote the protection and preservation of natural and cultural resources and discourage illicit trade in these items. The acquisition does not encourage unscientific excavations of archaeological materials. Considerations for the acquisition of unscientifically excavated or documented archaeological materials may include, but are not strictly limited to, prevention of random disposal that would distort the archaeological record, preservation of significant archaeological information, and promotion of public education about the value of archaeological investigations *in situ*.
2. The unique and special nature of items of particular cultural sensitivity is fundamental to decisions concerning such collections.
3. The museum accepts the importance of human dignity as it relates to human physical remains as a concern of many cultures. The museum is committed to acknowledging and respecting stakeholder perspectives regarding human remains, and, whenever possible, acting according to them.
4. The quality and completeness of the documentation accompanying an object is a decisive factor in considering it for acquisition. Objects with incomplete provenance will be given preference if there is evidence that suggests there is strong certainty that the object's context, origin, and history may be discerned through further research. Exceptions of this type should be made only for items after due diligence has provided assurance that the object was not illegally excavated or exported.
5. The museum wishes to maintain an open dialogue that enables the museum to work collaboratively and cooperatively with the international community toward our common goals. In this spirit, the museum may contact authorities from countries of origin or descendent communities if there is doubt about the legality of a potential acquisition.

Chapter 4

Implementing the Acquisition Policy

As the legal landscape summarized in Chapter 2 and the museum's ethical and institutional considerations served as the foundation of the policy drafted in Chapter 3, the same is true for the implementation of this policy. Meaningful policy adoption requires both a clearly articulated and customized policy as well as an equally well-defined and documented acquisition review procedure.

Thought should be given as to how to appropriately train staff regarding the museum's new policy for the acquisition of antiquated cultural property and archaeological material. In concert with this policy, the procedural steps outlined below may be modified to meet the museum's structure and operation. Procedural revisions may include updating the museum's broader collections management policy and sharing this policy online, updating or creating additional forms, checklists, or other documents that will be utilized during the review process, and allocating the various procedural responsibilities.

Overview of Procedural Review Process

The various steps outlined in Table 4.1 illustrate the full acquisition review process as described in Chapter 5. These steps are provided as a suggested structure but will likely be adapted to meet specific organizational requirements, although the underlying intent of these recommendations should be considered and adopted whenever possible. It should be noted that the acquisition process may be halted or delayed at any stage to request additional information.

Chapter 5 outlines all procedural steps in more detail. However, Step 3, the review of legal considerations, is broken out into separate chapters to allow for easy reference. Chapter 6 covers the legal review for domestic items, and Chapter 7 covers foreign material. Recommendations for performing additional due diligence are treated similarly. While general

Table 4.1: Proposed Procedural Review Process

Step	Task	Responsible Party
1.	Share acquisition guidelines and acquisition questionnaire.	Online, front desk/information, registrar, curator
2.	Review acquisition questionnaire, photographs of object, and photocopies of associated documentation.	Registrar's office, curator
3.	Review relevant U.S. and foreign legislation.	Registrar's office
4.	Prepare and distribute summary statement.	Registrar's office
5.	If determined minimally legally, ethically, and institutionally appropriate, request original documentation for review and make arrangements to examine object.	Registrar's office
6.	Perform additional due diligence research and prepare curatorial assessment statement.	Curatorial staff with knowledge of collection area, in consultation with outside experts as necessary. Registrar's office is available for consultation and should be notified if there is reason to request legal review.
7.	Collections Committee meeting and recommendation.	Collections Committee
8.	Approval of acquisition by appropriate authority.	Director, Board of Trustees, or other governing authority
9.	Final procedures to secure title. Accession object.	Registrar's office
10.	Document due diligence and decision-making process, regardless of decision.	Registrar's office
11.	Share acquisition information online.	Registrar's office
12.	Utilize acquisition for research and education.	All staff

due diligence steps are provided in Chapter 5, those that are specific to the item's origin are covered in Chapters 6 or 7.

Distribution of Responsibilities for Procedural Review

The procedural steps outlined in Table 4.1 delegate responsibility for the various procedural stages to different museum departments, thereby incorporating a system of checks and balances.

The approach advocates for the registrar's office to perform the initial review of documentation and legal restrictions, as these professionals are likely to be more knowledgeable about the laws governing acquisitions and title than other museum staff.

It is recommended that museums establish a procedure allowing representatives from curatorial departments to perform additional due diligence research. The museum must determine, in advance, who has the authority to designate curatorial staff to perform due diligence research and prepare a curatorial assessment statement (CAS). Curatorial staff should be selected for their knowledge of the particular type of item under review or the region from which it originated. Curators are more likely to be aware of red-flag issues, such as any history of illicit excavation and site destruction in the originating region, or problems that arose from similar acquisitions elsewhere. They are likely more familiar with the museum's holdings and are better able to gauge how the potential acquisition may enhance the existing collection's educational and programmatic potential than those working in registration. However, a curator should not be the sole judge, as the desire to acquire an item of particular personal interest may be a conflict of interest.

The monetary value of the property may also be considered when selecting the curatorial staff responsible for due diligence research. High-profile acquisitions or those requiring a significant financial expenditure may warrant the time of more senior staff, the involvement of more than one staff member, or a longer period of time for research. The registrar's analysis and curator's recommendation should therefore be distributed to the Collections Committee, or similar body, with sufficient time for curatorial staff to prepare the CAS.

The Collections Committee should ideally consist of representatives of various departments, including education. Museums may also wish to include public relations staff on the committee to identify any potential issues and develop communications strategies to mitigate any possible problems. The governing board should establish who in the museum has the ultimate authority for approving acquisitions: the director, chair of the board, or other governing authority. A valuation distinction is common, allowing for the director of the museum to approve acquisitions under a certain amount, but requiring the Board of Trustees to vote on items valued higher. However, if this distinction is made, the governing board should be informed of any acquisition that lacks irrefutable evidence showing adherence to all applicable laws, including state and foreign. Ultimately, the Board of Trustees, or other governing authority, is accountable for ensuring the institution's conformance with all legal requirements.

As a rule, museums should have on staff experts in the fields of study that have been identified as collecting priorities for the museum. It is however useful to develop a list of outside specialists,[1] who may serve on a special Acquisition Advisory Committee. The museum should contact these specialists when the list of experts is compiled to ensure their interest and willingness to advise the museum, and these consultants should be assured in writing that they will not be held accountable for any consequences that may result from acquisitions they advise on. The museum is responsible for ensuring the legality of the acquisition. These outside specialists may be called on to assist with problematic cases, such as items with incomplete or inconclusive documentation, or objects of a particular type or from a particular region subject to illegal excavation and/or trade.

Legal counsel with experience in cultural property law may also be sought to assist with such situations. Some museums may find it sufficient to schedule legal consultation once or twice a year and delay final decisions on potentially problematic acquisitions until after legal review. In addition, legal guidance should be requested in analyzing applicable state law to ensure basic criteria cover local restrictions, as discussed in Chapter 3, and to aid in the development of documents such as those described in Table 4.2.

These documents may provide an additional layer of protection and may be requested to support existing provenance information. Museums that have strict basic criteria for acquisition and require documentary

Table 4.2: Documents Likely Requiring Assistance of Legal Counsel

Legal Document	Purpose
Affidavit or Warrant of Provenance from a donor/vendor	Affirming the history of ownership, as provided, is presented as fact.
Donor Indemnity Agreement	A legal document for the donor to sign assigning all causes of action that may result in a dispute arising from the administration of the estate or after the disposition of property, which would enable the museum to seek damages from a dealer who sold the item to the donor under false pretenses.
Dealer Warrant and/or Indemnity Agreement	A document intended to release the museum from any expenses incurred by ownership claims made by a foreign country, tribal group, or other party.
Loan agreement with donor	A document that defers acquisition until a period of time after the item is widely exhibited and published, thereby meeting the open and notorious condition required of adverse possession, and possibly aiding in a laches defense against any future claims.
Document summarizing the legal review of a foreign country's cultural property laws	This is particularly applicable if the museum chooses to proceed with an acquisition that may be contrary to the country's export law.
Document summarizing the legal review of state laws governing acquisitions of archaeological resources	This is particularly applicable if the museum is considering anything transported from another state that may be potentially subject to ARPA.

evidence of conformity may not require such forms. All museums may nonetheless find it useful to have these documents available if the need arises, and the development of these documents should be considered a required step for museums who wish to define any exceptions to the basic criteria for acquisition. Legal counsel may also aid in the preparation of the museum's standard deed of gift form and bill of sale and other documents as discussed below.

Developing Additional Documentation

Various documents are utilized during the acquisition process and should be created and/or updated prior to implementing the review procedure. As mentioned, the acquisition policy established for antiquated cultural property and archaeological material should be included in the collection management policy, which should be shared online. The updated mission and ethics statements and scope of collections that were updated prior to writing this policy should also be included in the collection management policy, as should the procedural recommendations for implementing said policy.

In addition to the documents mentioned above that may require legal assistance to create, the museum's standard deed of gift form and bill of sale should be reviewed and updated as necessary. The bill of sale and deed of gift should incorporate language warranting that the donor or vendor attests that they have legal title to the item(s) and may legally transfer title and dispose of the item, and that all rights, title, and interest in, and all rights and interest associated with the object, including literary property rights and copyright, are being transferred to the museum. It should also state that, to the best of the donor or vendor's knowledge, the item was not exported, excavated, or transferred in violation of any U.S. federal, state, or local statute, international agreement, or foreign law.

The museum should draft an acquisition questionnaire and acquisition guidelines to share with prospective vendors or donors. The guidelines should summarize the museum's policies and review procedures pertaining to acquisitions and instruct the donor/vendor to complete the acquisition questionnaire and return it with photos of the objects under consideration and photocopies of associated documentation. Importantly, the guidelines should state that the museum reserves the right to contact authorities from the country or state where the item originated to ensure the legality of the item under consideration. Both documents should be available on the museum's website to enable transparency regarding the museum's acquisition policies and procedures. Table 4.3 outlines the various questions recommended for inclusion in the acquisition questionnaire.

Table 4.3: Recommended Information to Cover in Acquisition Questionnaire

1.	Date	
2.	Contact information	Name, address, phone numbers, and email addresses
3.	Owner	a. Are you the legal owner of the artifact? b. Are you the owner's authorized agent for the purpose of passing title? c. If so, who is the legal owner of the item? d. Are you aware of any other potential claims of ownership?
4.	Description	a. How many objects you wish to donate? b. Please provide a brief description of object(s) including materials, measurements, and condition.
5.	Value	a. What is the appraised value of object(s) you wish to donate? b. What was the date of appraisal? c. Please provide appraiser name and contact details.
6.	Provenance	a. What is the object's provenance (history of ownership)? Please provide as much specific information as possible, including names and contact information for prior owners, and dates of transfer. b. Where and how did the object come into the possession of the current owner? c. Please describe the circumstances surrounding the transaction. d. What was the date of acquisition? e. From whom was item acquired? (Provide name and contact details as known.) f. Describe the nature of your prior dealings with this individual or entity. g. Describe the manner in which the item's history of ownership was investigated (include whether you inquired about the history of the item's ownership or the possibility of the item being stolen, or if you relied on the word and expertise of the vendor). h. Was a database of stolen art checked before purchase? i. What was the price paid for the item? j. Describe when and how the object has been displayed by current or prior owners (i.e., included in publication or online, advertised for sale in auction catalogues, loaned to museums for exhibition, displayed in a home, etc.).
7.	For foreign items	a. What is the object's known country of origin? b. If country is not known, list likely country of origin. c. If known, list any intermediate countries where the object was transported. Indicate dates of exportation and importation, if known. d. Date of importation into the United States. e. Is the foreign export license from country of origin and other country it was exported from available? f. Is the U.S. Entry Summary (Form 7501) available? g. Is the accompanying Proforma invoice available?

Continued

Table 4.3: ***continued***

8.	For domestic items	a. If from inside of the United States, list the state where the item originated. b. If state not known, list likely state of origin. c. If known, list the owner of land where the object originated. d. If known, did the owner of the land permit removal of object? e. If known, what were the circumstances of this items acquisition or finding? f. Could the item have originated from federally or tribally owned or controlled land? g. Could the item have originated from state owned or controlled land?
9.	Documentation	a. What kinds of documentation are available? The following types of documents may provide acceptable evidence of provenance: will/inventory, photographic evidence, diaries, correspondence, auction or exhibition catalogues, bill of sale/sales receipt, excavation field notes, excavation permits, insurance record, publication in a reputable source, export license from country of origin, import/export documents from intermediate country, and/or U.S. customs documents, professional appraisals, condition reports, other. b. Are these documents originals or copies?
10.	Wildlife	a. Does the object incorporate fish and wildlife components? b. If yes, please indicate what permits or other documentation can be provided to demonstrate item's compliance with U.S. and foreign wildlife/endangered species laws, if known.
11.	Treatment	a. Has the artifact been treated with preservative chemicals, such as moth balls or insecticide? If yes, please explain.
12.	Financial support	The museum accepts a stewardship responsibility for donated objects that creates a financial obligation in perpetuity. Will a financial contribution be available to assist the museum with the care of these objects?

The acquisition questionnaire should be structured to provide sufficient room for response and comment, and check boxes may be included to facilitate answering Yes/No/Unknown questions. Vendors/donors should be instructed to complete the questionnaire to the best of their knowledge and provide additional sheets as necessary, and return it along with photos of the object(s) in question and photocopies of documentation. An example of acquisition guidelines and an acquisition questionnaire is provided in Appendix B.

If the registrar determines the item in question is of sufficient interest to review more closely, she or he may contact the vendor/donor to request original documentation be sent to the museum and to make arrangements for museum staff to examine the item in person. The vendor/donor should be given a custody receipt listing the objects and documents that have been temporarily transferred to the museum's custody and should include the vendor/donor's contact information, date of receipt, and a specific inventory or identification number to aid in tracking related information.

Lastly, the museum may wish to develop specific checklists to aid in the review of various procedural steps, such as review and analysis of foreign and domestic laws or additional due diligence procedures that are outlined in the following procedural chapters.

Chapter 5

Acquisition Review Procedures

This chapter provides procedural recommendations for the acquisition process for cultural material over 100 years old. An underlying goal of the suggested steps below is to help museum professionals navigate—in a way that protects both staff and the institution—the frequently confusing and politically charged legal landscape described in previous chapters. Risk assessment and mitigation strategies are integrated into the best practices provided for all stages of the acquisition review process. The greater degree of risk a museum is willing to take regarding acquisitions, the greater the need for risk management. Museums must be able to prove that a sufficient amount of research was done to ensure the legality of the acquisition and that the museum acted in good faith.

Preliminary Steps and Initial Review

The following section outlines procedures for the preliminary review of title based on the account of the donor and available documentation; this information is then analyzed in conjunction with legal considerations. These steps will help museum staff determine if good title to the item will pass to the museum.

Share Acquisition Guidelines and Acquisition Questionnaire

The museum should provide the acquisition guidelines and acquisition questionnaire to any person wishing to sell or donate items to the museum. The acquisition guidelines provide information on the museum's policies and review procedures pertaining to acquisitions and instruct the donor to complete the acquisition questionnaire and return it with photos of the object(s) under consideration and photocopies of associated documentation referenced in the questionnaire.

Review Acquisition Questionnaire, Photos of Object, and Photocopies of Documentation

The registrar will review the responses listed on the questionnaire along with copies or photos of the object and associated documentation. If, based on the responses on the acquisition questionnaire the registrar deems the item potentially appropriate for consideration, she or he may contact the donor and request original documentation be delivered to the museum and make arrangements for the appropriate staff person to physically examine the object.

If a museum chooses to have the item delivered to the museum with the original documentation, the donor/vendor should receive a custody receipt for all items delivered, listing associated documentation. Otherwise, the registrar may make arrangements to travel to examine the object outside of the museum. This examination may be made by the registrar, curator, and/or conservator, depending on the situation. Museums may wish to delay delivery of the item until after the relevant authority makes the decision to acquire the item, or after the Collections Committee recommends acquisition. Regardless of method, prior to obtaining title of the item, a physical examination of the object must be done to ensure authenticity and condition and to identify any red-flag issues.

Acceptable Forms of Documentation

While the primary objective of reviewing associated documentation is to determine the quality of the title being transferred, it is also important to determine the legality of the item's excavation and/or exportation. The following list includes the types of documentation acceptable as evidence of provenance.[1]

- correspondence
- wills or estate records
- diaries or travel journals
- photographic evidence
- bills of sale, receipts, canceled checks
- appraisals or authentications
- insurance records
- excavation field notes
- excavation permits
- publication in a reputable source
- exhibition catalogs
- auction catalogs
- condition reports

- foreign export licenses from country of origin or intermediate country
- U.S. Customs Entry Summary (Form 7501) and accompanying pro forma invoices
- certifications from Art Loss Register or other database of stolen property

Recommendations for analyzing the donor's account and associated documentation are provided in the due diligence section below. The registrar may contact the donor/vendor to request additional information or to provide clarification regarding acquisition questionnaire responses. The registrar may also arrange a meeting with the donor to record, with permission, a verbal account of provenance.

Review Relevant U.S. and Foreign Legislation

The registrar will review the donor's written and verbal account and the item's associated documentation, in conjunction with a review of legal rules restricting acquisition. The origin of the object determines the conditions restricting acquisition, including, but not limited to, the acceptable date of excavation or transfer, from what date provenance must be documented, and the required associated documentation. To aid in this review, legal review procedures are outlined in Chapter 6 for items originating within the United States and in Chapter 7 for those originating elsewhere. Based on this review, the registrar shall make a preliminary determination regarding the legality of acquiring the item and distribute this in the summary statement prior to the Collection Committee meeting.

The intent of this legislative review, including all applicable federal, state, and local laws, international conventions, and foreign laws, is to determine if the documentation provided and responses listed on the acquisition questionnaire provide sufficient evidence to legally acquire the item.

Although museums must perform due diligence research in all cases, as a rule, the greater degree of diligence exercised by the donor, the safer the acquisition. This is particularly true for items of a unique nature, known artist, or high value. Recommendations for evaluating the circumstances of the acquisition are covered in more detail below.

Not all considerations impacting the quality or completeness of title are included in the review process provided below; examples of these other factors include copyright and trademark considerations, possible claims by other family members or interested parties, and controlled wildlife restrictions, among others.[2]

Based on an analysis of the object's documentation, the account given by the donor and the review of applicable legislation, the registrar will write a summary statement indicating whether the museum has sufficient basis to determine if the item appears to meet the museum's basic criteria for acquisition. This statement should summarize the quality and completeness of documentation, U.S., international, and/or foreign rules impacting the legality of the acquisition, and whether the registrar believes unrestricted title may be passed to the museum. The summary statement should reference any state or foreign laws requiring additional analysis, including analysis required to acquire items exported in contravention of a foreign export law. It should also indicate if any additional documentation such as an affidavit or warranty is necessary. Furthermore, it should include any possible red-flag issues that require further research or specialized knowledge.

The registrar's office should circulate an agenda before the Collections Committee meeting, providing sufficient time for assigned curatorial staff to complete additional research and prepare a curatorial assessment statement.

Perform Additional Due Diligence Research and Prepare Curatorial Assessment Statement

An assigned curatorial staff member with sufficient knowledge of the region where the object originated or the culture associated with the item will be responsible for preparing a curatorial assessment statement (CAS) addressing any red-flag issues raised in the registrar's summary statement and bringing additional concerns and research to the Collections Committee. If the object falls outside of the field of expertise for current curatorial staff, outside specialists may be solicited to provide guidance to the staff member responsible for preparing the CAS.

The CAS should address compliance with the museum's ethical and institutional considerations, including how the object meets a specific need identified and articulated as a collecting priority for the museum. The curatorial staff should search the collections database to determine if any similar items are in the collection. If applicable, the report should note if the property is eligible for consideration due to any special factors, such as the application of "minor item" or "older collection" distinctions, as discussed in Chapter 3.

Additional due diligence research recommendations are described below, including: examining the artifact's physical characteristics, evaluating the quality of the documentation, identifying red-flag concerns based on the type of item or place of origin, considering the item's price, the reputation of and familiarity with the donor or vendor, and special considerations for online auctions.

Additional Due Diligence Research

In essence, the purpose of due diligence research is to avoid a claim of negligence that may result from taking inadequate measures to research the legality of an acquisition. The specific due diligence procedures undertaken are determined by the specifics of each case.

The following definition of due diligence provided in the 1995 UNIDROIT Convention is a useful standard for curatorial staff tasked with completing the CAS:

> In determining whether the possessor exercised due diligence, regard shall be had to all the circumstances of the acquisition, including the character of the parties, the price paid, whether the possessor consulted any reasonably accessible register of stolen cultural objects, and any other relevant information and documentation which it could reasonably have obtained, and whether the possessor consulted accessible agencies or took any other step that a reasonable person would have taken in the circumstances.[3]

The steps below are designed to assist staff with exercising the due diligence necessary to ensure the museum can prove it acted in good faith. Complete documentation of these procedures should be kept and made available at the Collections Committee meeting, and a summary of findings should be included in the CAS.

The following section outlining due diligence recommendations is loosely based on guidelines provided in two publications originating from the United Kingdom: *Combating Illicit Trade: Due Diligence Guidelines for Museums, Libraries and Archives on Collecting and Borrowing Cultural Material*,[4] and Paul Roberts's article "Barriers or Bridges? Museums and Acquisitions."[5] Marie Malaro's *A Legal Primer on Managing Museum Collections*[6] also provided useful recommendations.

Due Diligence Research Procedures

- examine artifact's physical characteristics
- evaluate the donor's account, documentation, and price of item
- consider the type of item, likely place of origin, and identify red-flag issues
- seek expert advice
- determine if object is listed in a database of stolen art

Examine Artifact's Physical Characteristics

The museum's conservator should assist curatorial staff with the examination of the artifact's physical characteristics, and the conservator's opinion should be included in the CAS. There are a variety of physical characteristics to consider, and the goal is to identify characteristics that support or refute the provenance information provided. The conservator should look for various means to date the object such as determining the type and relative age of any conservation or restoration treatment, as well as the style of mount, labeling, or other indications of prior ownership or display. The authenticity of these treatments, and of the object itself, should be evaluated. Further, the surface of the object should be analyzed to determine if there is any sign of soil indicating recent excavation of an archaeological item, or conversely, evidence of dirt and dust that have accumulated in crevices that may be indicative of the item being from an older collection.[7]

Evaluate the Donor's Account, Documentation, and Price of Item

The museum must consider the quality of the sources of information provided and have no reason to believe that the documentation provided was intentionally falsified or that the verbal account of the seller or donor is questionable. While items offered by donors not well known to the museum should be reviewed with particular caution, all potential acquisitions must be fully vetted. As a rule, the donor's account should not be accepted as fact without supporting documentation. However, an overabundance of documentation may also be suspect given the relative scarcity of provenance information historically traded, particularly for archaeological material from the United States. It is also important to keep in mind that documentation can be faked.

Purchases should be made from reputable vendors with whom the museum has previously dealt or whose reputation can be corroborated by trustworthy colleagues at peer institutions, although this is not always a fail-safe method of determining the integrity of a dealer. It is wise to check online sources to ensure the vendor is professionally affiliated and has not been party to illicit activity. For acquisitions offered to the museum from private parties for purchase, the reputation of the vendor the current owner acquired the item from, as well as the circumstances of that transaction, should be closely scrutinized. The most important rule of thumb is to ask questions and not simply accept the word of the dealer or the authenticity of the documentation, particularly if anything seems suspicious or deceitful.

The museum should be wary of donors who purchased an item without acquiring background information on the work's title or provenance or consideration of the vendor's character and professional reputation. Failure to do so should be viewed as red flags, as should any suspicious circumstances, such as transactions taking place in a country other than the United States or the country of origin, such as Switzerland or another country historically known for having less-than-stringent export laws.

The CAS should note whether the asking price for the item is in line with market value, as a cost lower than typical may indicate a problem with the title. Research on comparative sales may be done, with assistance from the registrar's office if necessary. If a donation, the museum must be assured the appraised price is not artificially inflated, as the museum should avoid the risk of enabling the donor to falsify tax documents and otherwise manipulate the market.[8] The appraisal price should be fair market value, "the price at which the property would change hands between a willing buyer and a willing seller, neither being under any compulsion to buy and sell and both having reasonable knowledge of the relevant facts."[9] Museums should be particularly suspicious of items appraised at a value just slightly under $5,000 or $20,000, as going above these valuation thresholds requires the donor to submit additional documentation to the IRS.

Acquisitions from online auction houses such as eBay require additional diligence. The United Kingdom Museums, Libraries & Archives Council website provides the following recommendations for buying from online sources: verify the identity of a seller, check the validity of the business name, check the reliability of contact details, avoid buying from those who only list a postbox address, and check the seller's track record by reading feedback from other buyers.[10] Before purchase, documentation and photos must be reviewed and legal restrictions and red-flag issues addressed.

In general, documentation provided as provenance should be original and specifically mention the item offered for acquisition. Vague statements of provenance must be substantiated. The museum should seek to obtain full contact information for all former owners and any galleries or auction houses that owned or housed the work. It is recommended that the museum research whether these owners and businesses existed and attempt to contact them to confirm the owner's claims. This step is particularly important for items considered for purchase or if the donor is not well known to the museum.[11]

While the names of prior owners and vendors serve as valid provenance because they provide information regarding the item's prior ownership and history, they do not necessarily offer the evidence necessary to show the item was legally exported from the country of origin, or intermediate country, or legally obtained within the United States. The same holds true if the proposed acquisition was mentioned in a publication; it can only serve as acceptable evidence of legal export if the date and content of the publication proves "its legitimate permanent export from the country of origin."[12]

If the authenticity of documentation is questionable, particularly export permits from the country of origin, then the museum may consult with representatives of the exporting country. A certification from the Art Loss Register accompanying the item under consideration is generally applicable only if the item is unique; the usefulness of such certification for most archaeological and ethnological material is limited.

If questions arise, the donor may be contacted for additional documentation or clarification, and/or to request a signed affidavit warranting the information provided.

Consider the Type of Item, Likely Place of Origin, and Identify Red-Flag Issues

Documentation review may uncover red-flag issues requiring further investigation, including suspicious circumstances surrounding the acquisition, the reputation of the current or prior owners or vendors, the price paid for the item, or gaps or incongruities in the item's history of ownership or transport. Unease may also result from the type of item or place of origin. Fortunately, many of the red-flag issues above can be researched online, which may uncover other areas of concern that require redress. Importantly, Internet research is increasingly being recognized by the courts as an essential part of due diligence research.[13]

Museum staff should perform general Internet searches on the object being considered for acquisition, using search terms indicating origin, material, and physical description as well as any other pertinent terms such as the name of the artist or collector. These general searches may indicate whether the material was illegally excavated, illegally exported, or stolen, and may also shed light on curatorial concerns such as rarity and comparable price.[14]

Indications of trouble and concern are, in large part, determined by the origin and type of item. As these concerns are origin specific, guidelines for looking into signs of trouble are provided separately for items originating outside and within the United States in the legal review in Chapters 6 and 7.

Seek Expert Advice

For items beyond the expertise of current curatorial staff, specialists may be retained to consult on the preparation of the Curatorial Assessment Statement. In addition, the museum should confer with other outside specialists, particularly if there is any indication that the type of object or the originating region is under threat from clandestine and destructive excavations of archaeological sites. These experts may be able to "advise both about geographical areas, particular types of item and possible sources of evidence of provenance" and "provide informed opinion about the reputation of the owner of the object."[15] The expert you choose to consult with is determined by her or his area of expertise. Additional suggestions of which authorities the museum may contact with questions are provided separately for items originating outside and within the United States in the legal review in Chapters 6 and 7.

Determine if Object Is Listed in a Database of Stolen Art

This step is increasingly cited in court rulings as indicative of proper due diligence, for both the owner of stolen property and good faith purchaser (see Table 5.1).

For uniquely identifiable items, particularly those created by a known artist or those of considerable value, a certification from the Art Loss Register[16] may prove useful if there is any question regarding the item's provenance.

However, for archaeological or ethnographic items lacking distinctive characteristics, this certification is not useful as the "owner" may not be aware of the item's existence or loss. A search of the free stolen property database, Trace,[17] should suffice for this type of material, although the museum may wish to confirm this distinction with legal counsel.

Table 5.1: Stolen Art Databases

Art Loss Register	The International Foundation for Art Research (IFAR) established the Art Loss Register (ALR) in 1976. ALR is the most commonly referenced international database of stolen art and antiquities. ALR staff compares data and photos submitted in an online form with stolen items in their private database. Upon completion, and after paying a search fee, an ALR search certificate is issued to confirm that, on the date the search took place, the item had not been reported stolen. IFAR also offers an art authentication research service for works of art whose authorship is in question.
Trace	Trace is the largest global online database of stolen, lost, seized, and recovered property. The site requires registration, but searching the database is free of charge. Searches require specific text or serial number. Owners of stolen goods list their stolen property for free, and law enforcement agents, insurance companies, and vendors such as dealers, auction houses, and pawn brokers may search the database.
FBI National Stolen Art File	The FBI National Stolen Art File is a computerized index of reported stolen art and cultural properties for the use of law enforcement agencies across the world. Items in this index are valued over $2,000 and uniquely identifiable. Requests for official searches must be made through a law enforcement agency involved in a criminal investigation, although the general public may search the database and use the FBI. gov tip line to report information on an identified item.

Other stolen art databases are available online, including private stolen art listings, foreign country databases such as the FBI site,[18] police listings, and WWII-era looted items.[19]

The Decision-Making Process

The following is one example of a decision-making process and may be modified to meet the structure and procedures needed by a particular institution, although it is recommended that responsibilities are broadly allocated and clearly defined and that the process provides sufficient checks and balances.

The Curatorial Assessment Statement, registrar's summary statement, acquisition questionnaire, and the object's associated documentation should be provided at the Collections Committee meeting. The records of donor/vendor correspondence, additional research, expert opinions, and photos of the item, if not the item itself, should also be available for review. If the curatorial staff member responsible for preparing the Curatorial Assessment Statement is not a regular member of the Collections Committee, that person should either be present at the meeting or available for consultation during the meeting; ideally, the same is true of consulting outside experts or legal counsel.

Based on this evidence, the committee will deliberate on the acquisition's compliance with the basic criteria for acquisition and ethical and institutional considerations listed in the museum's policy.

The committee should evaluate whether the acquisition would appear to sanction unscientific excavation or looting and should discuss whether an indigenous community or source country may hold an interest in this material, and if so, whether there is potential for a mutually beneficial outcome, such as joint ownership or scholarly collaboration. The benefit of acquisition for educational purposes, as well as the availability of staff resources to study and exhibit the object in a timely manner, should be addressed.

Importantly, the committee should perform the "newspaper test" on all acquisitions (i.e., how the acquisition would appear to the public if it was highlighted on the front page of a local, regional, or national paper).

The committee's recommendation will then be presented in writing by the registrar to the museum director. If the director has the authority to approve the acquisition she or he may do so or bring it to the attention of the Board of Trustees for discussion and vote. As mentioned, the Board of Trustees or other governing authority is responsible for ensuring the museum acts in accordance to the law, so any potential acquisitions that have substantial but not complete documentation regarding the item's legality should be brought to the board, as should items over a predetermined valuation.

The Collections Committee, director, or Board of Trustees, may choose to table the acquisition at any time, for any reason. These reasons may include, but are not limited to: requesting additional documentation; authenticating existing documentation, the donor's account, or the prior owners or vendors listed as evidence of provenance; contacting representatives of the country of origin or the state or tribal preservation office; further examining the object's physical characteristics; obtaining certification from the Art Loss Register; or consulting with other experts and/or legal counsel. Additional documentation to protect the museum may be sought, such as the affidavits, warranties, and indemnities discussed in Chapter 4 if the associated documentation is not sufficient to provide adequate evidence of the item's alleged provenance.

If the museum chooses to enter into a long-term loan agreement with the donor and defer acquisition until after a period of time has passed, as defined by the state's statute of limitations, as discussed below, the museum should immediately make plans to widely exhibit and publish the loaned item. However, these strategies should only be adopted if the item meets the basic criteria and ethical and institutional considerations and due diligence research do not raise any red-flag issues or raise any question regarding the donor/vendor's assertion of provenance or title. The decision-making process must be fully documented, regardless of whether the item is acquired, and files for items not acquired should be retained.

Final Procedures

If the acquisition is approved, the registrar's office should contact the donor or vendor to arrange for the transfer of title via a signed deed of gift or bill of sale. Museum staff must protect themselves—and their new acquisition—by ensuring that all documentation is in order, and informing the public of the addition to the collection. Standard accession procedures should be undertaken, as part of which the disclosure of the new acquisition should be made on the museum's website.

Adequate documentation of the legal review, due diligence research, and the deliberation process is necessary to prove that the museum acted in good faith in the event that it is ever accused of wrongdoing or if a claim is made on the item. Furthermore, publicly sharing information on the acquisition may commence the statute of limitations, after which the right to make a claim on the object may be barred.

The museum must only acquire objects for which it can be assured that, through the legal review process and additional due diligence procedures outlined above, the object is being transferred with a free and complete title, but there may be a time when an item in the museum's collection is claimed by an individual purporting to be the rightful owner. If this proves to be true, title remains with the last legal owner, although the museum has several means of possibly retaining the property, including adverse possession, statute of limitations (the discovery rule and the demand and refusal rule), and laches. These legal rules, discussed in Chapter 2, are intended to balance the rights of owners and good faith purchasers, and to enable the trade of property, but require that the museum perform all steps necessary to ensure they have made every possible attempt to ensure the item was held lawfully and thereby acted in good faith.

Documenting the Decision-Making Process

The acquisition file should be checked to ensure all applicable documentation is included. The accession file should include, but not necessarily be limited to:

- acquisition questionnaire
- photos of object
- registrar's summary statement
- Curatorial Assessment Statement
- associated documentation
- correspondence
- deed of gift or bill of sale
- signed or notarized affidavit warranting provenance, if applicable
- other documents prepared by legal counsel, if applicable
- summary of reviews of U.S. and international legislation of the country of origin or any intermediate country
- Collections Committee meeting notes
- any other documents that resulted from the due diligence process, including "information about factors specific to the type of item or place of origin"[20] gathered from:
    - documentation of director's or other governing body's approval;
    - country of origin and other websites including ICOM Red List, etc.;
    - other online material researched for indications of trouble;
    - statements from museum and outside experts regarding the item or its provenance, and evaluation of their counsel;
    - results of examination of the physical item;
    - search results from stolen art database(s) (Art Loss Register certification if item is uniquely identifiable object or of considerable value).
- If the Collections Committee decides against acquiring the object at any time during the process, the reasons for this should be noted and kept on file.
- A record of any publication of the new acquisition, as described in the next subsection, should also be included.

Share Acquisition Information Online

Following the acquisition, it is important to promptly disclose and disseminate information on the new donation or purchase. This is essential for a variety of reasons. The practice of quickly publishing relevant provenance information and an image of the item indicates the museum is acting in good faith and making efforts to communicate openly with interested stakeholders. Also, as discussed above, doing so is giving fair notice to any possible claimants who have a set period of time determined by state law to declare their ownership of the item.

The response to claims is beyond the scope of this publication, indeed, avoidance of this precise situation is a primary aim of this book. However, AAM recommends that any ownership claim be considered on its own merits and addressed respectfully and diligently. Also, museums should seek resolution directly with the claimant, or through a third party, when possible and prudent.[21]

Of paramount importance throughout the acquisition process is consideration of how the museum may use the object in a timely manner to further the museum's mission, serve the greater good, and educate the public. These goals can be achieved by utilizing cultural property in innovative educational, preservation, and public relations strategies discussed in Chapter 8. Prior to this discussion, Chapters 6 and 7 provide a framework for reviewing the item's conformance with the museum's basic criteria for acquisition and for performing additional due diligence research that is dependent on the item's origin.

Chapter 6

Reviewing the Basic Criteria for Acquisition of Domestic Cultural Property

This chapter provides a framework for reviewing the various laws restricting acquisition of domestic cultural property, specifically archaeological material over 100 years old, which originated within the United States. Steps concerning foreign property are covered in the next chapter. This legal review is just one step in the procedural recommendations outlined in Chapter 5. That chapter should be carefully reviewed, as the principles that ensure the legality of the item are incorporated throughout the acquisition review process. This is true of questioning the provenance, reviewing the associated documentation, and performing the necessary diligence and final procedures. However, for domestic items, especially archaeological material, the item's provenience—the specific find site and circumstances regarding the find—is of particular significance.

The common law rules for property described in Chapter 2 generally prevail for cultural property originating within the United States. Ethnographic material is commonly covered by standard legal rules governing the exchange of property, although some may fall under the cultural item categories and be subject to repatriation under NAGPRA. For archaeological material, the owner of the land will generally hold title to items found embedded or firmly affixed in the soil. When considering acquiring archaeological or ethnographic material originating within the United States, the first step should be to determine, to the best degree possible, from which state the item likely originated and then investigate the type of land the object was found on—federal, tribal, state, municipal, or private. The date and circumstances of the original find should also be established, when possible.

After an archaeological resource is removed from its original context, it is often difficult to determine its precise origin with certainly and even more difficult to ascertain who owned or controlled the land where the object was found. The object's associated documentation and the vendor or donor's account are the primary means for determining the object's provenience. The physical characteristics of the object may also enable the museum to determine the originating state or tribal affiliation. Responses provided on the acquisition questionnaire, coupled with a review of documentation, cover the primary provenance and provenience questions needed to establish compliance with the museum's basic criteria for acquisition.

The format of the legal review is based on the basic criteria for acquisition for domestic cultural property, as defined in Chapter 3, and provided in Table 6.1. While these basic criteria primarily cover legal restrictions, they also incorporate professional standards and ethical distinctions.

These basic criteria for acquisition are covered individually below. Tables listing each basic criterion include what material is restricted under those criteria, or what could be considered as exceptions, along with the documentation required to ensure that the criterion is met. These tables are followed by a discussion of the considerations and procedural recommendations. Criteria 1 and 2, items originating from federal and tribal lands respectively, are discussed jointly as most legal restrictions apply to both (see Tables 6.2 and 6.3).

Federal regulations applying to burial items and archaeological material include the Antiquities Act of 1906,[1] the Archaeological Resources Protection Act of 1979 (ARPA),[2] and the Native American Graves Protection and Repatriation Act of 1990 (NAGPRA).[3] The curatorial value of the material should be weighed against the burden of caring for

Table 6.1: Examples of Basic Criteria for Acquisition of Domestic Cultural Material

1. Require permits and other documentation for archaeological resources or cultural items originating from federally owned or controlled lands after 1905.
2. Require permits and other documentation for archaeological resource or cultural items originating from tribally owned or controlled lands after 1978.
3. Have reasonable assurance the object was not illegally excavated from lands controlled by any state or municipal statutes (particularly those relating to burial sites or restricting the sale, transport, or possession of archaeological material) after the effective date of applicable statutes.
4. Have reasonable assurance that any cultural items as defined by NAGPRA (human remains, associated or unassociated funerary objects, sacred objects, or objects of cultural patrimony) are being transferred with clear right of possession.
5. Require evidence the owner of the private property where the archaeological material originated permitted the excavation, removal, and transfer of the object and renounced further claims to the object, with possible exceptions as defined by the museum.

Table 6.2: Domestic Basic Criterion 1: Federally Owned Land after 1905

Required permits and other documentation for archaeological resources or cultural items originating from federally owned or controlled lands after 1905.

Material Restricted	Documentation Required
a. Objects of antiquity from archaeological sites, historic, or prehistoric ruins or monuments from federally owned and controlled lands between 1906 and 1978 (covered under the Antiquities Act).	a. Federally issued Antiquities Act granted by the secretaries of the interior, agriculture, or army to institutions. Record of title given to institution responsible for excavation, or transfer of title from that institution to current donor. Memorandum of Agreement (MOA) with federal agency outlining curation standards in line with Federal Regulation 36 CFR 79.
b. Archaeological resources excavated from federally owned and controlled lands after 1979 (covered under the ARPA), defined as: any material remain of past human life or activities which are of archaeological interest ... (include[ing], but not limited to: pottery, basketry, bottles, weapons, weapon projectiles, tools, structures or portions of structures, pit houses, rock paintings, rock carvings, intaglios, graves, human skeletal materials, or any portion or piece of any of the foregoing items that are at least 100 years of age. [16 U.S.C. 470bb]	b. Federally issued ARPA permit required. MOA, with federal agency outlining curation standards in line with Federal Regulation 36 CFR 79. (Note: Title is retained by the federal government.)
c. Native American cultural items, including human remains, associated or unassociated funerary objects, sacred objects, and objects of cultural patrimony, which show a relationship of lineal descent or cultural affiliation to a federally recognized tribe, that were excavated after 1990 on federally owned or controlled lands. (Cultural items covered under NAGPRA are defined below under Criterion #4.)	c. Federally issued ARPA permit required. Evidence of tribal consultation, including written plan of action and/or notice of intended disposition. Depository agreement with tribal government. (Note: Title is retained by the federal or tribal government.)

the material in the manner specified in federal regulation 36 CFR 79, as discussed in Chapter 2.[4]

A museum should proceed particularly cautiously if there is any reason to believe the antiquity originated from a burial or archaeological site on federal or tribal land. If it is likely that the item originated from federal or tribal lands, review the documentation to determine the earliest record of recovery.

Table 6.3: Domestic Basic Criterion 2: Tribally Owned or Controlled Land after 1978

Required permits and other documentation for archaeological resources or cultural items originating from tribally owned or controlled lands after 1978.

Material Restricted	Documentation Required
a. Archaeological resources over 100 years old as defined above under "b" in Criterion #1, which were excavated from tribally owned or controlled lands after 1978 (covered under the ARPA).	a. Federally issued ARPA permit required. (Note: Title is retained by federal government MOA with federal agency outlining curation standards in line with Federal Regulation 36 CFR 79.)
b. Native American cultural items, including human remains, associated or unassociated funerary objects, sacred objects, and objects of cultural patrimony that show a relationship of lineal descent or cultural affiliation to a federally recognized tribe, which were excavated after 1990 on tribally owned or controlled lands. (Cultural items covered under NAGPRA are defined below under Criterion #4.)	b. Federally issued ARPA permit required. Evidence of tribal consultation, including written plan of action and/or notice of intended disposition. Depository agreement with tribal government. (Note: Title is retained by the federal or tribal government.)

If the item was in a known collection prior to 1906, it may be safely collected. However, the NAGPRA future applicability rule may apply, as discussed below.

If the material was collected between 1906 and 1978 from federal lands, then the Antiquities Act of 1906 is relevant. The material may be legally acquirable if it is accompanied by a federally issued permit. The Antiquities Act permitted institutions to excavate on federal lands. Therefore, the transfer of this material should generally be from another institution, or there should be a record of the material being deaccessioned and title transferred to the individual offering the material.

Archaeological material collected from federal or tribal lands after 1979 require a permit under ARPA. The ownership of ARPA-permitted archaeological material is retained by the federal or tribal government.

Items thought to be from federal or tribal lands that were not obtained during federally or tribally permitted excavations require documentation that they were in a private collection by 1978 or earlier. Archaeological resources obtained from federally or tribally owned or controlled lands after 1979 cannot be considered for acquisition. Even temporary custody of these items is a liability.

The laws of the probable originating state(s) should be reviewed to determine whether the material is restricted by state law. The following sources may be referenced to determine if the excavation or transfer of archaeological material is constrained by state law:

- Arrowheads.com Indian Burial Laws, last updated 2010.[5]
- The National Conference of State Legislatures' State Historic Preservation Legislation Database, last updated in 1999.[6]
- The compilation of State Repatriation, Reburial, and Grave Protection Laws, updated in July 1997.[7]
- Carol L. Carnett's *A Survey of State Statutes Protecting Archeological Resources*, published in 1995.[8]

As three of these four resources date from the 1990s, the appropriate state historic preservation office (SHPO) website may be referenced for more current restrictions. The National Conference of SHPOs website has direct links to SHPO websites.[9]

As discussed in Chapter 2, it is a federal crime under ARPA to handle archaeological material in a way that violates any state or local law, which may include activity on private property. The registrar should be familiar with state regulations governing archaeological material before proceeding with acquisition. Furthermore, other statutes designed to protect property more broadly should be considered, such as theft, trespass, conversion, transport of stolen goods, among others, and the museum should find no indication of violation of said laws.

It should be presumed that burial and archaeological sites on publicly owned lands are always protected. While burial sites are nearly always covered by state law, protection given to other archaeological resources varies by state.

Local laws may impact archaeological materials on private property, particularly if the property is listed on the state register of historic places or if there is a preservation restriction or easement on the property. If this seems likely, the museum should search online for the municipality's historic commission or planning department, which often provides links to the town by-laws. The by-laws may indicate whether there are specific statutes specifying the disposition of archaeological material resulting from intentional or chance finds on public or private property. Local laws often also impose restrictions against disturbing cemeteries and burials (see Table 6.4).[10]

The four types of cultural property as defined by NAGPRA are: human remains (affiliated and unaffiliated), burial objects (associated and unassociated), sacred objects, and objects of cultural patrimony showing a relationship of lineal descent or cultural affiliation with a federally recognized tribe.[11] These categories are defined in Table 6.4. Human remains that cannot be shown to be held with a clear right of possession should not be acquired. Other NAGPRA-defined cultural items held

Table 6.4: Domestic Basic Criterion 3: In Violation of State or Local Law

Have reasonable assurance the object was not illegally excavated from lands controlled by any state or municipal statutes (particularly those relating to burial sites or restricting the sale, transport, or possession of archaeological material) after the effective date of applicable statutes.	
Material Restricted	**Documentation Required**
Ensure the circumstances of acquisition in no way indicate that the material was acquired in violation of any state statute, such as those concerning theft, conversion, or trespass. Special attention should be given to material that may have been excavated from a burial or cemetery on public or private property, or archaeological material from publicly owned land. Laws may also restrict material originating from a locally or state recognized historic private property, or a property that has a preservation restriction or easement placed on it, although these restrictions are atypical.	• Documented findings from search of one or more of sources of information on state laws, or state historic preservation office website. Specific attention should be given to material resulting from burial sites, cemeteries, and state or municipally owned properties. • Depending on the specifics of the case (date of find, etc.), either search online and document findings or request the donor signs a statement indicating that, to the best of his or her knowledge, the excavation and transfer of the item was lawful. • The state archaeologist should be consulted with questions.

without clear right of possession should generally not be acquired unless the curatorial value of the material outweighs the administrative burden of NAGPRA compliance and/or the museum wishes to act as a temporary depository to facilitate repatriation.

Cultural items and human remains, as defined by NAGPRA, that were collected from federal or tribal lands after 1990, require that tribal permission be obtained for excavation, which is done according to procedures set forth by ARPA and NAGPRA. Ownership of this material is retained by the tribal government.

Criminal penalties exist for illegal trafficking in human remains or cultural items obtained from federal or tribal lands after 1990, in violation of NAGPRA. Knowingly selling, purchasing, using for profit, or transporting for sale or profit, "human remains of a Native American without the right of possession to those remains as provided in the Native American Graves Protection and Repatriation Act" or "any Native American cultural items obtained in violation of the Native American Grave Protection and Repatriation Act" will result in fine and imprisonment upon conviction.[12]

The 2007 NAGPRA future applicability rule applies to all cultural materials as defined by NAGPRA. The acquisition of NAGPRA-defined cultural items requires museums to comply with the procedural requirements of NAGPRA, including summarizing holdings, public notification, consultation with tribal representatives, and possible repatriation. Museums should be careful to review an item's associated documentation to ensure, to the best extent possible, that possession of the item was "obtained with the voluntary consent of an individual or group that had authority of alienation."[13] In addition to weighing the curatorial value of material potentially falling under NAGPRA, the museum should refer to the ethical considerations incorporated into their acquisition policy to guide in the decision-making process (see Table 6.5).

No federal laws prohibit the excavation and removal of archaeological materials from private lands so long as the landowner consents and doing so does not violate state or local law. However, items obtained from burials or cemeteries, even on private lands, are generally protected by state statute.

Archaeological material reportedly collected from private lands as part of a professional archaeological investigation should be accompanied by required permits, stamps, and verification forms, in addition to field notes and documentation.

For material originating from private property but not resulting from scientific excavation, the museum should confirm that the owner of the property approved the excavation, collection, and removal of the object. Receipt of a signed and notarized affidavit releasing the object from further claims, or other document transferring title, is recommended.[14] Additional documentation is required if the person donating archaeological material is not the owner of the land on which the material was found. In that case, the donor should provide documentation that the object's title was legally transferred by the owner of the land.

Unfortunately, the documentation of title transfer for archaeological material found on private lands has not always been recorded. The museum may consider acquiring the material if the donor warrants that the material came from private property with the property owner's permission, so long as doing so is not prohibited by state or local law and no red-flag issues or indication of legal wrongdoing are observable.

Under common law, title to stolen property is void at the time of theft and cannot be transferred, even to a good-faith purchaser. The adverse possession doctrine provides for a degree of security; the action that starts the running of the statute of limitations is often the true owner discovering (or being able to discover) the whereabouts of her or his stolen property. However, it is unlikely that the original owner of unprovenienced archaeological material can be discovered or contacted because of the nature of archaeological material. This does not negate the fact that the owner of the stolen property—who, for most U.S. archaeological

Table 6.5: Domestic Basic Criterion 4: NAGPRA Cultural Items and Human Remains

Have reasonable assurance that any cultural items and human remains as defined by NAGPRA (human remains, associated or unassociated funerary objects, sacred objects, or objects of cultural patrimony) are being transferred with clear right of possession.

Material Restricted	Documentation Required
The NAGPRA future applicability rule is triggered by the nature of the cultural material; the date and origin of collection are not factors.*	Documentation showing the item to be held with right of possession.
a. Human remains: the physical remains of the body of a person of Native American ancestry. The term does not include remains or portions of remains that may reasonably be determined to have been freely given or naturally shed by the individual from whose body they were obtained, such as hair made into ropes or nets. For the purposes of determining cultural affiliation, human remains incorporated into a funerary object, sacred object, or object of cultural patrimony must be considered as part of that item. [43 CFR 10.2 (d)(1)] b. Associated funerary objects: objects that, as a part of the death rite or ceremony of a culture, are reasonably believed to have been placed with individual human remains either at the time of death or later, and both the human remains and associated funerary objects are presently in the possession or control of a federal agency or museum, except that other items exclusively made for burial purposes or to contain human remains shall be considered as associated funerary objects. [25 USC 3001 (3)(A)]	Right of possession is defined as: Possession obtained with the voluntary consent of an individual or group that had authority of alienation. The original acquisition of a Native American unassociated funerary object, sacred object, or object of cultural patrimony from an Indian tribe or Native Hawaiian organization with the voluntary consent of an individual or group with authority to alienate such object is deemed to give right of possession of that object. ... The original acquisition of Native American human remains and associated funerary objects that were excavated, exhumed, or otherwise obtained with full knowledge and consent of the next of kin or the official governing body of the appropriate culturally affiliated Indian tribe or Native Hawaiian organization is deemed to give right of possession to those remains. [25 USC 3001 (13)]
c. Unassociated funerary objects: objects that, as a part of the death rite or ceremony of a culture, are reasonably believed to have been placed with individual human remains either at the time of death or later, where the remains are not in the possession or control of the federal agency or museum and the objects can be identified by a preponderance of the evidence as related to specific individuals or families or to known human remains or, by a preponderance of the evidence, as	With the exception of human remains, other NAGPRA-defined cultural items (funerary, sacred, and patrimonial) may be acquired unless they originated from federal or tribal lands after 1990. However, it is likely that such items will be repatriated. In such cases, the museum may wish to serve as a temporary depository to facilitate repatriation, so long as doing so

Continued

Table 6.5: ***continued***

Material Restricted	Documentation Required
having been removed from a specific burial site of an individual culturally affiliated with a particular Indian tribe. [25 USC 3001 (3)(B)] Those funerary objects for which the human remains with which they were placed intentionally are not in the possession or control of a museum or federal agency. [43 CFR 10.2 (d)(2)(ii)]	does not provide material incentive to current looting and does not violate state law. It is advisable to consult with tribal groups before doing so.
d. Sacred objects: Specific ceremonial objects that are needed by traditional Native American religious leaders for the practice of traditional Native American religions by their present-day adherents. [25 USC 3001 (3)(C)]	The acquisition of human remains of indigenous origin is not recommended for procedural and ethical reasons. The NAGPRA rule on culturally unidentifiable/unaffiliated human remains requires museums to follow a procedure that may result in repatriation to tribal groups living in the area where the human remains were found.
e. Object of cultural patrimony: An object having ongoing historical, traditional, or cultural importance central to the Native American group or culture itself, rather than property owned by an individual Native American, and which, therefore, cannot be alienated, appropriated, or conveyed by any individual regardless of whether or not the individual is a member of the Indian tribe or Native Hawaiian organization and such object shall have been considered inalienable by such Native American group at the time the object was separated from such group. [25 USC 3001 (3)(D)]	The museum may wish to develop a policy that enables it to take custody of such material to facilitate repatriation. This safe-harbor provision may be utilized in the event that the donor intends to discard material otherwise.

*All extracts are from: http://www.nps.gov/nagpra/TRAINING/GLOSSARY.HTM.

material, is the owner of the land where the material originated—still maintains title. Without absolute proof that this person conveyed title to the current possessor, the museum cannot be certain that title is transferrable to the museum, and runs the risk that the acquisition will be claimed by the rightful owner (see Table 6.6).

The scenario described above presents something of a quagmire for museums. Ultimately, the decision to acquire an item with unknown provenience, but with a sufficiently long and credible provenance or resulting from unscientific methods on private property, is governed by ethics, risk management, the museum's mission, and professional affiliation.

To aid in the decision-making process, museums should note in their acquisition policy if exceptions will be made for U.S. material found to be lacking complete documentation placing title in the current holder, or material with incomplete or unknown provenience, and if so, from what date the item's provenance needs to be documented. The degree of provenance should ensure that sufficient time has elapsed so that acquisition

Table 6.6: Domestic Basic Criterion 5: From Private Property

Require evidence the owner of the private property where the archaeological material originated permitted the excavation, removal, and transfer of the object and renounced further claims to the object, with possible exceptions as defined by the museum.

Possible Exceptions	Documentation Required
While this publication does not recommend a museum acquire an object lacking complete provenance and provenience information, a museum may choose to identify possible scenarios where exceptions may be made. Legal counsel should be consulted when establishing these exceptions. Below are two examples of exceptional circumstances a museum may incorporate into their basic criteria for acquisition if doing so is in line with their institutional and ethical considerations and upon approval of the museum's legal counsel and governing board:	• Archaeological material reportedly collected from private lands as part of a professional archaeological investigation should be accompanied by permits, stamps, and verification forms, in addition to field notes and documentation.
• A "minor item" is an object (or group of objects) valued at $5,000 or less. This term applies to material originating from within and from outside the United States. The $5,000 value is based on the definition of objects covered under the National Stolen Property Act. • An "older collection" is an antiquity with documented provenance dating back to at least 1978. The 1978 date is intended to predate material subject to the 1979 Archaeological Resource Protection Act (ARPA).	• Exceptions made for material meeting the "minor item" or "older collection" definition must be accompanied by a credible account of provenance from a trustworthy donor, and, as a result of due diligence, there is no indication of the item's illegal or questionable nature, including objects that appear "freshly excavated, from a 'hot' area, or a 'hot' category of item."[1] Furthermore, the museum may accept the object so long as no federal, state, or local laws are identified that prohibit transfer. A signed affidavit warranting the item's provenance should be required. Ideally, this document should indemnify the museum by stating the museum will not be held responsible for any expenses incurred by ownership claims made by a tribal group or other party.

will not provide material incentive for current unscientific excavations or looting. Furthermore, the provenance documentation must date back far enough to at least indicate that the statute of limitations period has passed.

Deference to the statute of limitations for unprovenienced material may not be considered the most ethically sound practice, nor is such a procedure easily implemented. In contrast, 1978 is a practical cutoff date, as it predates ARPA. If a museum chooses to make exceptions for items from older collections with indisputable pre-1979 provenance, it may do so only if no federal, state, or local laws are identified that prohibits transfer. Furthermore, the museum must ensure that no other legal or ethical considerations are brought to light while performing due diligence research, as disregarding such signs of trouble could be viewed as evidence of recklessness. The museum may wish to make this exception only for minor items valued less than $5,000.[15] Some museums opt not to purchase such items, but accept them only as gifts, presumably to not offer financial incentive to continued archaeological site destruction but to provide a safe harbor for such items. Material with questionable provenience or incomplete provenance should be accompanied by a notarized statement warranting the object's provenance. Ideally, the statement should include an indemnity clause, which will hold the museum harmless for any expenses arising out of a potential claim for the item. Legal counsel should be consulted when preparing this document and the museum's governing board should approve such cases.

Refer to Table C.1 in Appendix C for an outline of the types of U.S. restricted cultural property and the documentation required to ensure compliance with basic criteria.

Due Diligence Procedures Specifically for Domestic Items

In addition to performing the legal review steps provided above, the museum should perform additional research to ensure the item is legally and ethically acquirable and to prove that the museum has performed the due diligence necessary to show they are acting in good faith. Most due diligence procedures are outlined in Chapter 5, but the following may be considered for items specifically originating from the United States.

Consider the Type of Item, Likely Place of Origin, and Identify Red-Flag Issues

Museums should proceed cautiously if there is any reason to believe the antiquity originated from federal or tribal land. It is often not clear where archaeological material originated, and it is difficult to prove an item's provenance after its removal. To help determine if the material originated from federal or tribal lands, museums may review the National Atlas of the United States of America.[16] Certain types of American Indian cultural material are more likely to originate from federal or tribal lands, such as material affiliated with current or prehistoric cultures in the American Southwest, particularly the Four Corners area. As mentioned in Chapter 5, museums should search online for reports on illegal activity and archaeological site destruction in the area where the item originated.[17] Also, the Indian Burials and Sacred Grounds Watch website provides a list of federal and state protected Indian burial grounds and mounds.[18]

Seek Expert Advice

For U.S. material, it is advisable to contact the state (SHPO) or tribal (THPO) preservation officer or state archaeologist for additional information. The national conference of state historic preservation officers' website links directly to state SHPO websites, which often provide direct links to the state laws governing archaeological material.[19] The National Association of Tribal Historic Preservation Officers[20] and the National Association of State Archaeologists[21] also provide useful contact information and guidelines.

Considering the type of item and likely place of origin, identifying red-flag issues, and seeking expert advice are critical steps to performing due diligence, but the initial, widely applicable steps outlined in Chapter 5 should also be carried out.

Chapter 7

Reviewing the Basic Criteria for Acquisition of Foreign Cultural Property

This chapter provides a framework for reviewing the various laws restricting acquisition of cultural property, aged over 100 years, originating outside the United States. The basic criteria for acquisition incorporate specific legal rules governing this property, as well as ethical distinctions recommended by professional standards, including the application of 1970 as the date after which increased scrutiny is required. Analysis of the applicability of legal rules is just one step in the procedural recommendations outlined in Chapter 5. The entire procedural review process should be followed as the principles that ensure the legality of the item are incorporated throughout the recommended process. This is true of questioning the provenance, reviewing the associated documentation, and performing the necessary diligence and final procedures.

For foreign material, the country from which the item originated, the type of the material, and the date(s) of export/import and associated documentation are of primary significance.

The museum should be able to ascertain the country of origin for objects from outside the United States. If the country of origin is not verifiable for items lacking proof of presence in the United States before the museum's cutoff date, the museum should not acquire them. After the country of origin and any intermediate countries of transit have been identified, staff should endeavor to determine whether exportation or ownership of the object is restricted.

Export or ownership restrictions vary with country of origin. Table D.1, Restrictions Governing the Cultural Property of Foreign Countries, located in Appendix D, is intended to assist museum staff in making an initial determination, but the additional resources provided below and in Appendix F, Additional Resources, should be consulted directly as museums should confirm that the status of the country of origin, or intermediate country, has not changed. The table in Appendix D lists those countries that are: impacted by any U.S. legislation, treaties, executive agreements, or customs embargos; have accessible cultural property laws and the dates of those laws; have accepted or ratified the 1970 UNESCO Convention and the date of that action; have been identified as a the source country for particular types of items subject to illicit trade; or have historical resources in danger of destruction.

Restrictions applying to material of foreign origin include the Cultural Property Implementation Act; the Pre-Columbian Monumental, Architectural Sculpture or Murals Act; customs embargoes, U.S. treaties and executive agreements, other criminal laws such as the National Stolen Property Act, and, in some cases, state laws and the Archaeological Resources Protection Act.

The format of the legal review is structured around the basic criteria for acquisition, as defined in Chapter 3. While these basic criteria primarily cover legal restrictions, they also incorporate professional standards and ethical distinctions (see Table 7.1).

These basic legal criteria are covered individually below. Tables show each basic criterion along with restricted material and required documentation, along with a discussion of the criteria and procedural recommendations. Criteria 5 and 6, regarding the laws restricting exportation and claiming ownership, are discussed jointly below.

Table 7.1: Examples of Basic Criteria for Acquisition of Foreign Cultural Material

1.	Require evidence the object is not covered under the Regulation of Importation of Pre-Columbian Monumental or Architectural Sculpture or Murals Act.
2.	Require evidence that the object is not designated as restricted under the Convention on Cultural Property Implementation Act.
3.	Have reasonable assurance the object was not reported stolen by a foreign country.
4.	Have reasonable assurance the item was not subject to U.S. customs import restrictions or sanctions.
5.	Require evidence the object was not exported after November 17, 1970 in violation of export or ownership laws of the country of origin and/or the country where it was last legally owned.
6.	Have reasonable assurance the item was not exported before November 17, 1970 in violation of foreign law, with possible exceptions as defined by museum.
7.	Require evidence the object was legally imported into the United States after November 17, 1970. Have reasonable assurance the item was legally imported prior to this date, with possible exceptions as defined by museum.

The Pre-Columbian Monumental, Architectural Sculpture or Murals Act may restrict acquisition.[1] This act impacts pre-Columbian monumental or architectural sculpture or murals originating from one of the following countries: Bolivia, Belize (British Honduras), Columbia, Costa Rica, Dominican Republic, Ecuador, El Salvador, Guatemala, Honduras, Mexico, Panama, Peru, or Venezuela. Care should be taken when acquiring pre-Columbian objects from these countries. The documentation listed in Table 7.2 is required for importation. It is advisable to confirm that the customs papers authorizing export from these countries are authentic. The U.S. customs publication notes that "'country of origin' is intended to mean the country where the sculpture or mural was first discovered" (see Table 7.2).[2]

Material acquired from countries party to agreements, including bilateral agreements or memorandums of understanding and emergency agreements, under the Convention on Cultural Property Implementation Act (CPIA)[3] should be considered restricted and may be subject to forfeiture. As of February 21, 2011, designated cultural property from the following countries is currently restricted under the CPIA: Bolivia, Cambodia, China, Colombia, Cyprus, El Salvador, Guatemala, Honduras, Iraq, Italy, Mali, Nicaragua, and Peru. Canada's Bilateral Agreement was applicable between April 22, 1997 and April 9, 2002. New restrictions may be added to this list and existing restrictions may expire or be terminated at any time; therefore, the list should be reviewed for updates.[4] Not all cultural material originating from these countries is restricted.[5]

Table 7.2: Foreign Basic Criterion 1: Pre-Columbian Monumental or Architectural Sculpture or Murals

Require evidence the object is not covered under the Regulation of Importation of Pre-Columbian Monumental or Architectural Sculpture or Murals Act.

Material Restricted	Documentation Required
Pre-Columbian monumental or architectural sculpture or murals from Bolivia, Belize (British Honduras), Colombia, Costa Rica, Dominican Republic, Ecuador, El Salvador, Guatemala, Honduras, Mexico, Panama, Peru, or Venezuela exported after June 1, 1973.	• A certificate, issued by the government of the country of origin of such sculpture or mural, in a form acceptable to the secretary of the treasury, certifying that such exportation was not in violation of the laws of that country; or • Satisfactory evidence that such sculpture or mural was exported from the country of origin on or before June 1, 1973; or • Satisfactory evidence that such sculpture or mural is not an article subject to the Pre-Columbian Monumental Act and regulations.[1]

Material covered under CPIA may be permitted entry into the United States if the documentation noted in Table 7.3 is available and authenticated (see Table 7.3).[6]

The museum must perform the necessary research to prove they made a concerted effort to determine if the item was reported stolen from a foreign country. The resources provided in Chapter 5 may be used for this purpose, particularly the FBI National Stolen Art File, which provides images of uniquely identifiable items that have been reported stolen art and cultural properties from across the world.

The U.S. government entered into four treaties and executive agreements to facilitate the recovery and return of specific categories of objects stolen from federal, state, or municipal governments or their instrumentalities. Mexico, Peru, Guatemala, and Ecuador all have such agreements with the United States, which are intended to facilitate cooperation on the recovery and return of archaeological, historical, and cultural properties.[7] These materials included items of outstanding importance to the national patrimony of both countries, including objects and artifacts of the pre-Columbian indigenous cultures, art objects and religious artifacts from the colonial period, and pre-1920 documents of historical importance taken from official archives.[8]

These treaties do not appear to restrict importation; rather, its intent is to assist with the recovery and return of objects that fall into these

Table 7.3: Foreign Basic Criterion 2: Convention on Cultural Property Implementation Act

Require evidence that the object is not designated as restricted under the Convention on Cultural Property Implementation Act.

Material Restricted	Documentation Required
As of November 2010, designated cultural property from the following countries was restricted: Bolivia, Cambodia, China, Colombia, Cyprus, El Salvador, Belize, Guatemala, Honduras, Iraq, Italy, Mali, Nicaragua, and Peru. (Canada's Bilateral Agreement was applicable between April 22, 1997 and April 9, 2002.)	• A certificate or other documentation issued by the government of the country of origin certifying the exportation was not in violation of laws of that country, or • Satisfactory evidence that the designated material was exported from the state party not less than ten years before the date of entry and neither the person for whose account the material was imported (or any related party) contracted for, or acquired an interest in the material more than one year before the date of entry, or • Satisfactory evidence that the designated material was exported from the state party on or before the date that the material was designated under 19 USC §2604.[1]

categories. The treaties permit legitimate international commerce in art objects, consistent with both countries' laws and regulations so an analysis of the laws of these countries is necessary to ensure that the exportation of the object in question was done legally (see Table 7.4).

A rather volatile class of potential restrictions is made up of U.S. customs embargoes. As of February 21, 2011, sanctions include material from the Balkans, Belarus, Myanmar, Côte d'Ivoire, Cuba, Democratic Republic of the Congo, Iran, Iraq, Lebanon, North Korea, Somalia, Sudan, Syria, and Zimbabwe.[9] The list is subject to change and it is prudent to confirm that an embargo was not in effect at the time the object left its country of origin. It is important to note that if an item is seized by customs authorities, even if a U.S. court would not have upheld such seizure, the process of retrieving the detained item requires court judgment and, therefore, a large financial burden (see Table 7.5).

Table 7.4: Foreign Basic Criterion 3: Stolen Property

Have reasonable assurance the object was not reported stolen by a foreign country.

Material Restricted	Documentation Required
• Items inventoried by a museum of similar institution or objects that may be traced to official excavation site in the country of origin. (CPIA limits restriction to countries that are signatories to the UNESCO Convention.)	• Printed results of database for stolen art (Trace.com for most items, and a certificate from Art Loss Register for unique and/or valuable items).
• Pre-Columbian property from Mexico, Peru, Ecuador, and Guatemala stolen from federal, state, or municipal governments or their instrumentalities, covered under U.S. treaties and executive agreements.	• Documented investigation of website(s) from the likely country or countries of origin, the UNESCO website, and a general Internet search for key words describing the item.
• Other known items reported stolen.	

Table 7.5: Foreign Basic Criterion 4: U.S. Customs Restrictions

Have reasonable assurance the item is not subject to U.S. customs import restrictions or sanctions.

Material Restricted	Documentation Required
Nearly all property from Iraq, Cuba, Iran, Sudan, and Myanmar, as well as material from the Balkans, Belarus, Côte d'Ivoire, Democratic Republic of Congo, Iraq, Lebanon, North Korea, Somalia, Syria, and Zimbabwe.	• Documentation required by U.S. customs and/or website, or customs documents showing the item was imported prior to effective date of the sanction or is not subject to said sanction.

Museums should review whether the country of origin had a law in place that may restrict ownership or exportation. For items from countries with cultural property laws, determine the effective dates of the cultural property laws of the countries of origin and any intermediate countries. The laws should also be reviewed to determine if the item under consideration is indeed restricted, and if so, what associated documentation is needed. Establish whether the item's corresponding documentation certifies that the item was not exported in violation of international cultural property laws and if it was exported after the museum's specific cutoff date (i.e., 1970) (see Tables 7.6 and 7.7).

Foreign material should generally be accompanied by foreign export licenses from the country of origin and any intermediate country. Museums should review these forms, or other available documentation, to determine if the information provided on the export license is consistent with the museum's understanding and supports the donor's account of provenance. This information includes the item's description, date of exportation, declared value, and country of origin.

Several sources of information are available to assist the museum staff in its investigation of foreign property laws. These include: the International Cultural Property Ownership & Export Legislation Database provided by the International Foundation for Art Research[10]; The UNESCO Cultural Heritage Laws Database[11]; the Handbook of National Regulations Concerning the Export of Cultural Property[12]; and the Collection of Legislative Texts Concerning the Protection of Movable Cultural Property.[13]

Some museums choose to honor cultural property laws only for signatories of the 1970 UNESCO Convention on the Means of Prohibiting and Preventing the Illicit Import, Export and Transfer of Ownership of

Table 7.6: Foreign Basic Criterion 5: Foreign Export/Ownership Laws, Post-1970

Require evidence the object was not exported after November 17, 1970 in violation of export or ownership laws of the country of origin and/or the country where it was last legally owned.

Material Restricted	Documentation Required
Items restricted by foreign law.	• Documented findings from search of IFAR and UNESCO databases. • Associated documentation that provides concrete and irrefutable proof of the object's legal exportation after the museum's established cutoff date (foreign export license from country of origin as well as any other intermediate country).

Table 7.7: Foreign Basic Criterion 6: Foreign Export Laws, Pre-1970

Have reasonable assurance the item was not exported before November 17, 1970 in violation of foreign law, with possible exceptions as defined by museum.	
Possible Exceptions	**Documentation Required**
While this book does not recommend that a museum acquire an object lacking complete provenance and provenience information, a museum may choose to identify possible scenarios where exceptions may be made. Legal counsel should be consulted when establishing these exceptions and these should be approved by the governing board. Possible exception may be granted for items lacking export documentation, so long as the export did not violate a foreign law clearly deeding ownership of the item at the time of export. Determination requires legal counsel. Below are examples of exceptional circumstances a museum may incorporate into their basic criteria for acquisition if doing so is in line with its institutional and ethical considerations, and upon approval of the museum's legal counsel and governing board: • Possible exceptions include "minor items" and "adequately publicized works," so long as doing so does not conflict with state law. • Items valued over $5,000 require notification of the foreign country's representative.	• Documented findings from search of UNESCO and IFAR databases and other sources. • If the law clearly deeds ownership of the material to the country of origin, then the item must not be acquired unless it is determined to be a minor item and is accompanied by a notarized affidavit warranting the provenance of the object and releasing the museum from harm. • If the law does not clearly deed ownership of the material to the country of origin and merely prohibits export, the item may be acquired, although a signed affidavit warranting provenance is advisable. The museum may also only want to make this exception for minor objects, and/or after contacting country of origin representatives. • Any material acquired in contravention of foreign law must be accompanied by a credible account of provenance from a trustworthy donor, and, as a result of due diligence, there is no indication of the item's illegal or questionable nature, including objects that appear "freshly excavated, from a 'hot' area, or a 'hot' category of item."[1] Furthermore, the museum must ensure that no federal, state, or local laws are identified that prohibit transfer. A signed affidavit warranting the item's provenance should be required. Ideally, this document should indemnify the museum by stating the museum will not be held responsible for any expenses incurred by ownership claims made by a tribal group, or other party. • Other required documentation may include export permits; independent appraisal for valuations under $5,000, documented analysis of foreign property law (including statement by legal counsel), and state law search documentation.

Cultural Property. If that is the case, the museum should be familiar with which countries have accepted or ratified the convention.[14] This distinction would not provide protection against customs seizure, or against liability under NSPA or ARPA.

If exportation was after the museum's cutoff date, and authentic documentation does not exist regarding the item's legal export, it should not be acquired.

If the exportation was before the museum's cutoff date but after the effective date of the international cultural property law, and reliable documentation does not exist regarding its legal export, the museum may wish to further study the law to conclude whether the law clearly states ownership of the cultural property or if only the export of the property is prohibited.

Under certain conditions and with legal counsel, museums may wish to consider exceptions for material exported before the museum's cutoff date in violation of a country's export law that does not clearly declare ownership. Importantly, this is an ethical distinction that requires pre-consideration and preapproval of governing authority and legal counsel. If the museum wants to distinguish between an ownership and export law, legal counsel should be obtained to make the final determination, after an initial analysis is performed by the registrar. The legal analysis should be retained as part of the item's acquisition review documentation. The museum may determine that such exceptions should be made only for minor items valued less than $5,000. The museum must also determine if the state where the museum is located has a statute prohibiting receiving property stolen from another country and bringing it into the state while knowing the property was stolen, as violation of the state law may be considered a federal violation.

Such exceptions should not be made indiscriminately; the museum should consider the public's perception of such a distinction. Obviously, a simpler and safer approach would be to defer to the export laws of the country of origin and not acquire the item. However, the questions in Table 7.8 and in Jessica Darraby's 2006 publication, *Art, Artifact and Archaeology Law*, may be helpful for museums seeking to determine the likelihood of a foreign cultural property law being upheld in U.S. courts.

Museums are advised to contact embassies or consulates for current laws or for clarification prior to proceeding with an acquisition based on such a distinction. As a rule, museums should assume that a patrimony law will be upheld in U.S. courts and always consider the perception of the acquisition by the public and source country and whether state statutes may pose additional restrictions.

The U.S. customs publication states that, "[a] violation of a foreign export control law is not in and of itself grounds for U.S. Customs and Border Protection action."[15] An item must generally be covered by the Convention on Cultural Property Implementation Act or the Regulation of Importation of Pre-Columbian Monumental or Architectural Sculpture or Murals in order for an artifact to be considered cultural property by

Table 7.8: Questions to Aid in Determining the Enforceability of Foreign Patrimony Laws in U.S. Courts[1]

1.	Does the [foreign] state have a "law" purporting to declare ownership in tangible personal property?
2.	Has the law been translated into English?
3.	Does an unequivocal right to ownership of property survive translation?
4.	Does the law relate to the property at issue?
5.	What are the effective dates of the law?
6.	What acts did the [foreign] state exercise incident to ownership?
7.	Did export regulations applicable to the property exist, and if so, what [are the] effective dates?
8.	Was the property transshipped through other countries? If so, those laws and export regulations may need to be investigated.

U.S. Customs.[16] However, the customs publication continues by stating: "Of course, if a violation of U.S. law occurs, the articles may be subject to seizure and forfeiture under U.S. law regardless of foreign law."[17] This qualification refers to the enforcement of the National Stolen Property Act, which has enabled other county's laws to be upheld in U.S. courts and the potential application of state laws in conjunction with ARPA to enforce foreign property laws.

The customs publication also notes that "Cultural property and other articles, which were stolen, smuggled into the United States, or not declared to CBP are subject to seizure and forfeiture under the CBP and related laws."[18]

Therefore, imported property should have U.S. customs paperwork, specifically U.S. Customs Form 7501[19] and accompanying pro forma invoice[20] if applicable, indicating that its origin and value were appropriately declared. Of particular importance is the review of the date of entry (line 7 of Form 7501), importer (line 26 of Form 7501), country of origin (line 10 of Form 7501 and pro forma invoice, if applicable), and declared value (line 32 of Form 7501 and pro forma invoice, if applicable). The museum should ensure that the description of the merchandise, date of entry, importer, valuation, and country of origin is in line with reported provenance and the museum's understanding. If the item is being purchased by the museum, they should note if the value listed is consistent with the agreed upon purchase price. If not, determine if the value listed was the amount the importer paid[21] (see Table 7.9).

Table E.1, Basic Criteria for Foreign Cultural Property, located in Appendix E, outlines the types of foreign restricted and endangered

Table 7.9: Foreign Basic Criterion 7 U.S. Importation

Require evidence the object was legally imported into the United States after November 17, 1970. Have reasonable assurance the item was legally imported prior to this date, with possible exceptions as defined by the museum.	
Possible Exceptions	**Documentation Required**
Possible exceptions include "minor items," so long as doing so does not conflict with state or federal law.	Request donor signs an affidavit and warranty of title, and request dealer, if purchased, to sign an indemnity agreement.

cultural property, as well as the types of documentation necessary to prove that such objects may be legally acquired.

DUE DILIGENCE PROCEDURES SPECIFICALLY FOR FOREIGN ITEMS

Consider the Type of Item, Likely Place of Origin, and Identify Red-Flag Issues

For foreign material, the museum must give additional consideration to items originating from certain areas in the world, often subject to war and poverty, where the archaeological record is under great threat.[22] The museum should ask: "Is a country's cultural patrimony in jeopardy from pillage of archaeological and ethnological materials and/or other illegal actions and how will the acquisition affect such activity?"[23] and address this question within the context of world events. No one resource is available for searching for regions of world that are currently experiencing or recently experienced extensive looting and site destruction.

The UNESCO World Heritage in Danger List includes sites that the World Heritage Committee decided to include on the List of World Heritage in Danger in accordance with Article 11 (4) of the 1972 World Heritage Convention. The World Heritage Committee can inscribe on the list properties whose protection requires "major operations" and for which assistance has been requested.[24]

Importantly, the ICOM Red List includes cultural goods most affected by looting and theft from Africa, Latin America, Iraq, and Afghanistan. These objects are protected by legislation and banned from export. While the object types provided do not constitute an exhaustive list of all threatened cultural resources, it is a useful starting point.[25]

The museum should proceed with caution with any item appearing on the Red List. For listed items, the museum is advised to seek expert advice, including legal counsel and/or representatives from ICOM, UNESCO, and the government authority that has restricted export of such materials. Although it is possible that these types of items may be legally acquired, it is necessary to ensure that doing so is legally and ethically appropriate and that evidence exists that they were exported prior to the enactment of any foreign cultural property law.

Seek Expert Advice

Those with specialized knowledge on the cultural property in question may be consulted to determine there is any indication that the type of object or the originating region is under threat from clandestine and destructive excavations of archaeological sites.

The International Cultural Property Ownership & Export Legislation Database provided by the International Foundation for Art Research[26] and the UNESCO Cultural Heritage Laws Database[27] provide contact information for the government officials that the museum should contact regarding the legality of acquiring the work. Consulate and UNESCO staff may also be helpful. Foreign consular offices in the United States can be searched through the U.S. Department of State.[28] UNESCO field offices may also be contacted.[29]

Considering the type of item and likely place of origin, identifying red-flag issues, and seeking expert advice are critical steps to performing due diligence, but the additional steps outlined in Chapter 5 should also be carried out.

Of paramount importance, the museum must also consider how to make use of the object, in a timely manner, to further the museum's mission, serve the greater good, and educate the public.

Chapter 8

The Future of Museum Collecting: Motivated by Preservation and Education

As previous chapters have illustrated, the collection of cultural property has become increasingly complicated, difficult, and risky because of the growing number of legal and ethical concerns affecting acquisitions and the unprecedented rigor with which these concerns have been interpreted. Indeed, it may no longer be possible for museums to amass comprehensive collections of archaeological material and antiquities because of the expansive number of restrictions.[1] A further complication is negative media coverage of the role that museums have purportedly played in the destruction of archaeological heritage. Given this situation, it is often difficult to remember that all parties are ostensibly working toward the same goals: the preservation of cultural heritage and the advancement of knowledge.

An Opportunity, Not an Obstacle: Increased Involvement of Stakeholders and the Importance of Education

In the current context, museums must expand their vision of the traditional museological model, which has historically endorsed the growth of physical collections and the importance of ownership and preservation in perpetuity. Today, museums should consider how these objects—accessible either through ownership or loan—can advance our understanding and appreciation of the world in which we live. A complimentary and essential condition to this approach is a more expansive and holistic view of what a museum's responsibility is to a broad array of constituencies. This inclusive philosophy advocates for increased involvement of a wide variety of stakeholders in museum operations, including education, research, exhibitions, and curation as well as acquisitions. The current unsettled ethical and legal landscape governing acquisitions presents a positive opportunity for museums to focus resources and energy, normally spent on building collections, toward serving, educating, and involving the public and other stakeholders.

There are myriad creative, collaborative, and novel approaches that museums can adopt in this regard. Whether as part of a collection or on loan, antiquities and archaeological material are significant vehicles for public education. They also serve as international ambassadors that can establish cross-cultural dialogue, not only between museums and the countries and cultures from which the objects originated, but also between members of our increasingly multicultural society. These items are primary ties to our common cultural heritage; the value of having access to these objects and learning from them cannot be expressed in monetary terms. We need archaeological material and antiquities in our museums so that, given the appropriate circumstances, we can make connections with our broader world and our common cultural heritage.

The educational value inherent in exposing visitors to objects from around the world is greatly increased when innovative educational and exhibition strategies are integrated, and this is true of items in current collections, future acquisitions, and items on loan. Access to and preservation of the tangible and intangible aspects of cultural heritage should be considered the fundamental goals, enabling a better understanding of our shared past and providing opportunities for collaborative, communicative, and respectful relations with source countries and descendant communities. Ownership is not a prerequisite. Indeed, the ability to borrow objects is a privilege the museum community would be unwise to jeopardize. Maintaining positive and cooperative relations with those entities who control loans, particularly representatives from source countries and descendant communities, is therefore essential.

As recent negotiations between museums and source countries have shown, mutually beneficial solutions are obtainable by means of communication, compromise, and collaboration. While future dialogues may result in select items from museum collections being returned to source countries or communities, the positive results of these returns, such as increased access to cultural material through loans and opportunities for collaborative research and programming may outweigh the negative, but only if these negotiations are regarded as opportunities rather than obstacles.

When NAGPRA was introduced in 1990, members of the museum community voiced resistance and concern that their American Indian collections would be emptied by repatriations. Although the consultations have often been emotionally charged and challenging, they have resulted in better relations between museums and descendant communities. Innovative strategies such as co-curation agreements were developed to enable the merging of traditional care and standard museum care practices. Many involved in the NAGPRA process feel the positive outcomes of increased understanding of collections and native cultures have surpassed the loss of returned items.[2]

These cooperative efforts offer more than increased knowledge; they may also serve as positive publicity for museums. As an example, to replace a totem pole repatriated to the Cape Fox Corporation, on behalf of the Saanya Kwaan Teikweidi Clan in 2001, the Harvard University Peabody Museum of Archaeology and Ethnology commissioned Nathan Jackson, master carver of the Tlingit tribe, to create a new totem pole from a tree donated by the tribe. The new pole, installed in the Hall of the North American Indian, "symbolizes a new bond between the descendants of Gash village and the museum."[3] The repatriation and subsequent commission from a traditional artist illustrates the continuance and vitality of the Tlingit culture, reaffirming that the items shown in the Peabody Museum represent the present and future as well as the past. Examples such as this show the variety of collaborative options available to museums that look beyond the traditional ownership paradigm. Improving stakeholder relationships and advancing knowledge are the primary motivations, and these goals translate into positive public relations for the museum.

Integral to our understanding of global cultural heritage is knowledge of context and history, often garnered through scientific and scholarly analysis. When considering an acquisition of antiquated or archaeological material, museums should therefore weigh its potential for advancing knowledge through public access and scholarly investigation against any unintentional damage the acquisition may have on the global historic record. If ownership of an item would endorse, or appear to endorse, further destruction of archaeological sites, the item should not be acquired. Museums may, however, consider how to utilize such items already within their collection to educate the public about the problems of archaeological site destruction and illicit trade, particularly if opportunities exist for collaboration with the countries of origin or descendant communities.

Museums are well positioned to educate the public regarding the importance of an item's provenance and provenience in understanding our cultural heritage. By illustrating how artifacts are direct links to understanding our past, museums provide opportunities to promote the fundamental role museums have played and continue to play in preserving cultural heritage. By doing so, museums may also inform the public, particularly private collectors who may one day wish to donate their collection to the museum, of the ever-changing legal and ethical landscape governing collecting.

Museums have many resources for educating the public about the impact of the trade in unprovenanced or unprovenienced antiquities and the value of archaeological documentation. These may include, but are not limited to: their own collections and those on loan, interactive videos, audio tours, handheld devices, photos, graphic representations of data, maps, archaeological site documentation, online exhibitions and forums, lectures, email news bulletins, sponsored professional archaeological excavations, publications, plaster casts, publicly viewed conservation efforts, traveling exhibitions, models, and all manner of educational programs. Permanent collections in particular offer a powerful means of communicating with the public, although their potential has seldom been realized due to their typical, static, and decontextualized manner of exhibition.

Exhibitions

The traditional manner of display of antiquities—decontextualized works of art, rather than the materialization of an intangible religious or cultural heritage—does not reflect changing moral conceptions. The emphasis on an object's formal characteristics is in many ways a disservice to the public, the country or culture of origin, and our more complete understanding of the object. When we view these objects purely in terms of aesthetic or monetary value, we are apt to lose connection with the original meaning of the object—unintentionally communicating to the public that archaeological and/or cultural context are not intrinsically tied to the object's significance or value.

In many museums, the litmus test of a work of art is dependent upon its ability to stand alone, stripped of contextual information.[4] But as we consider an object in a museum, we must remember that "the ability to stand alone says less about the nature of the object and more about our categories and attitudes."[5] There is no doubt about the importance of preserving antiquities and archaeological resources; their provenience, context, contents, purpose, and creator's intent are integral to fully appreciating and understanding them. We must be diligent, however, about safeguarding more than just "specimens of human ingenuity and creativity"[6] and make clear to the public that it is not simply the antiquities that are endangered but also our ability to understand our common past.

Funerary objects—sarcophagi, tombs, headstones, mummies, urns, human remains, and other objects taken from burial sites—require particular attention in their presentation. The collection and display of funerary objects as works of art has been a long-standing practice for museums, and there is a growing acknowledgment that "the unique and special nature of human remains and funerary and sacred objects is recognized as the basis for all decisions concerning such collections."[7]

Because of the morally and politically charged nature of press coverage regarding museums' involvement in the trade of illicit antiquities, the public is growing increasingly sensitive to the items exhibited in museums and the manner in which these items are displayed and interpreted. As a result, the traditional decontextualization of burial items may be misconstrued as a disregard for deceased individuals or their descendants. Museums should evaluate the manner of exhibition of burial items and establish justification for their display by developing educational programs that articulate the special nature of these collections.

The same is true for objects considered culturally sensitive or sacred by indigenous groups. The 2006 AAMD Guidelines for the Treatment of Sacred Objects "calls on museums to consult with indigenous groups to determine what works might fall into this category and to accommodate the wishes of these groups as far as possible in displaying, conserving and even discussing these works on museum labels and in catalogs."[8]

Museums must keep in mind that the residual impact of colonialism may unwittingly influence the display and interpretation of material culture, particularly items that hold cultural significance for present-day communities. Mark O'Neill, head of Glasgow Museums and professor in the Department of Museum Studies at the University of Leicester, encourages museums to "embrace rather than ignore the fact that the superiority of white, male, western, academic perspectives is being challenged, particularly in their authority to speak about and on behalf of 'the other'."[9] O'Neill also remarks that, whenever possible, the "historical and/or contemporary voices from the cultures which produced the objects" should be incorporated into the interpretation.[10]

In 2002, the Declaration on the Importance and Value of Universal Museums endeavored to defend the right of museums to retain items acquired through methods considered unethical by current standards.[11] Implicit in this statement is the relegation of prior collecting methods as merely a product of the past and one warranting no further comment or acknowledgment. Museums should not be reticent about publicly acknowledging their history. A comparison of prior and current collecting methods may illustrate that once acceptable behavior is no longer ethically or legally tolerable.

Transparency

Sharing information about the item's ownership history and its origins communicates to the public the often fascinating story of how the ancient object before them made its way to the museum. It is currently not standard practice to publicly share provenance information, with the possible exception of the year the object was acquired and the name of the donor or sponsored fund. Sincere efforts should be made to be more open with this information while respecting privacy concerns.

A bold use of provenance information was integrated into a unique exhibition strategy adopted by Boris Wastiau, curator at the Royal Museum for Central Africa in Tervuren, Belgium, in the 2000 exhibition "ExitCongoMuseum: A Century of Art With/Without Papers."[12] This exhibition highlighted the museum's renowned collection of African art, which had largely been collected—some would say stolen—from the Belgian Congo during the colonial period. Items from the collection were accompanied by archival documents and photos illustrating the previously unspoken history of exploitation.

A similarly revealing approach was incorporated in an exhibition curated by the Wadsworth Athenaeum in "Acquiring Art in the 90s: The Inside Story," which discussed the museum's acquisition policy and procedures while unveiling the inner workings of the normally concealed museum world.[13] This strategy could be a useful means of informing the public about the processes that museums go through when acquiring works of art, including antiquities and archaeological material, and could provide insight into the challenges faced by museum professionals in this world of constantly shifting legal and ethical considerations.

Collaborative Endeavors

Through their exhibitions, museums may also wish to share stories about ongoing dialogues with source countries, particularly when the narrative can speak of successful examples of compromise and collaborative resolution. Such a strategy is utilized in the M. H. de Young Museum's exhibition of murals from the Mayan city of Teotihuacan. The series of seventy mural fragments—the largest anywhere outside Mexico—were bequeathed to the museum without information pertaining to the date of removal of the objects, although evidence showed that they had been in California since the late 1960s, indicating the museum could legally obtain ownership. Despite this, and perhaps because the museum realized that the size, scope, and importance of this donation distinguished it as Mexico's cultural patrimony, the museum worked with Mexican cultural representatives to establish a program allowing for joint conservation and care of the murals. In addition, the museum returned two-thirds of the mural collection to Mexico after the conservation program was completed.

In exchange for shared ownership of the murals, the Mexican institute sent specialists in the conservation of pre-Columbian monumental sculpture to San Francisco to work on the conservation of the murals and train staff from the de Young Museum. The conservation treatment took place in the galleries so that the public could witness this historical cooperative effort. The series of murals are now exhibited at the de Young Museum and the introductory wall text gives an eloquent overview of the seventeen-year process of establishing the unprecedented 1981 agreement reached between the Fine Arts Museums and the Instituto Nacional de Antropología e Historia de México.[14]

The M. H. de Young Museum has another important object within their American pre-Columbian gallery that illustrates their efforts to work collaboratively with foreign governments. A Mayan limestone stela from an indeterminate area near the border of Mexico and Guatemala was donated to the art museums of San Francisco with documentation that it had been in the United States prior to 1971. The museum contacted both Guatemala and Mexico to see if either country objected to the museum acquiring the piece.[15]

As part of their good-faith efforts to work collaboratively with their Latin American neighbors to protect their cultural patrimony and archaeological heritage, the museum proposed a multi-part strategy. First, the stela would be described in detail in the exhibit and in at least one illustrated publication, and this description would include the stela's history, care, and research that preceded its acquisition and information pertaining to the problems and issues concerning national patrimony today. Second, the stela would be recognized as part of the national heritage of both Guatemala and Mexico and, if new evidence regarding the original location of the stela was discovered, the museum would be open to renegotiating with the country of origin, would declare the object as part of the that country's patrimony, and would explore options such as joint ownership. Last, the museum would join with the countries' cultural ministries to collaborate on projects to help preserve and bring world recognition to the national patrimony of these countries, such as sharing conservation resources to protect sites and collections, encouraging joint scholarship, producing collaborative exhibitions and publications, or promoting exchanges or personnel or resources. Through their good-faith efforts the museum strengthened its relationship with Guatemala and Mexico, which both approved the museum's acquisition of the stela.[16] In both cases, the de Young Museum's cooperative efforts also provided good public relations material for its own use.

Another inspiring example is the de Menil Collection's conservation of a series of Byzantine frescoes stolen from a Greek Orthodox church near Lysi, Cyprus. Northern Cyprus was occupied by Turkish forces in 1974, at which time the region's churches were looted of their religious paraphernalia, frescoes, and mosaics. Many pieces were severely damaged in the process. The Menil Foundation of Houston, with the permission of the Cypriot government and church authority, purchased the frescoes on behalf of the Church of Cyprus. The foundation began a two-year conservation effort with the goal that, when the political climate improved, the frescoes would return to their home country. Owned by Cyprus, and on long-term loan to the Menil Foundation, the paintings represent the "only intact Byzantine frescoes in the entire western hemisphere."[17] The frescoes were installed in a new building purposely designed for them by architect François de Menil. The museum, open since 1997, is frequently cited as a positive example of museum and source community relations.[18]

The examples above illustrate efforts various museums have undertaken to ensure the laws and concerns of source countries are respected. Working openly with source country representatives, these museums found collaborative solutions that went beyond what was required by law to advance the common goal of preserving cultural heritage.

Education: Strategies for Using Unprovenienced Items

While consulting with source countries and descendent communities holds great potential for collaborative opportunities, it is not necessary for implementing successful education and preservation strategies. These strategies can be utilized regardless of whether they have documented provenance and provenience.

Museums may wish to disclose the inherent limitations of what can be learned from items with questionable or unknown provenance or archaeological contextual information. Much of what is known about an unprovenienced item must be derived from its comparison with documented archaeological collections.[19] Illustrations of how unanswered questions could have been resolved through proper excavation would promote increased public appreciation of contextual data and awareness of what information is lost when an object is unscientifically removed.

Harvard University's Semitic Museum adopted a novel approach to working with a collection of items with limited provenience. In 1995, the museum acquired over 1,300 objects from Cyprus, dating from ca. 2300 BCE to 700 CE. These items were collected in the 1860–70s by General Luigi de Palma Cesnola, the U.S. consul to Cyprus. While there, Cesnola gathered an enormous collection of Cypriot antiquities, including ceramic vessels, lamps, figurines, and stone, glass, and metal objects, which were amassed without regard to their archaeological context. Cesnola's collection formed a large part of the Metropolitan Museum of Art's original collection. A portion of this collection and its associated archives were transferred to Harvard. Through an analysis of Cesnola's written account and knowledge of the region's archaeological resources, the Semitic Museum recontextualized the archaeological material by illustrating the likely origins of various material types on a map of Cyprus. This strategy allows a museum visitor to tie items to their origins, while reinforcing the importance of context and other archaeological data to facilitate a full understanding of the object.

Education: Strategies for Using Provenienced Items

For items with known provenience, it may not be prudent to share site-specific information with the public for fear that this may further expose archaeological sites to looting and unscientific collecting. However, indicating site-specific contextual information without reference to the site's precise location is still useful and allows the visitor to gain a better understanding of how archaeological excavations are performed and why context and site stratigraphy are important. Because such a large percentage of antiquities within museums have not been professionally excavated, the application of this educational strategy is often not possible. Although this is an unfortunate product of our past collecting activities, it makes those objects that were scientifically excavated even more valuable for public education.

By sharing specific contextual information about how and where an object was found *in situ*—through pictures, videos, and other visual and multi-sensory means of communication—we may be able to increase visitors' comprehension of the object and its origin. Accompanying images and select facts about what was, or may still be learned, from an excavation, can increase visitors' appreciation of the potential for knowledge presented by professional archaeological excavations without overwhelming the viewer with written documentation.

The Museo Tumbas Reales de Sipán[20] (Museum of the Royal Tombs of Sipán), located in Lambayeque, Peru, is a noteworthy example of how magnificent items can be beautifully displayed while highlighting the importance of archaeological context. This modern museum was built to showcase the treasures unearthed from the relatively undisturbed archaeological site of the Royal Tombs of Sipán. The museum incorporates a wide variety of interpretive strategies that contextualize the archaeological finds and shed light on the life and afterlife of the Moche culture. Full-scale reproductions of the Lord of Sipan's tomb and the various other smaller tombs are displayed, showing replicas of layers of significant archaeological finds in their original context.

The original items are displayed separately, highlighting their physical beauty and allowing the viewer to understand the cultural meaning of each object. Photographs and site maps documenting the archaeological investigation tie the item to the original context. A life-size, automated diorama showing the Lord of Sipan and the members of his court who were buried with him as they would have appeared in life further contextualizes the individuals and cultural property that were uncovered during scientific excavations. Exhibitions at the start of the museum are dedicated to educating the public about the science of archaeology and the Moche culture, and a final museum exhibit focuses on the threat to archaeological sites within Peru and what museum visitors can do to protect this heritage. Interactive computer displays and audio visual presentations round out this comprehensive educational experience.

Moving Forward

Museums should use the current climate as an opportunity to educate the public about the importance of provenance and provenience information, the negative impact illicit trade in antiquities has on our ability to understand our common cultural heritage, and the important role museums continue to play in preserving this heritage. Museums must, however, ensure that their acquisition policies and procedures are in line with professional and legal standards—and their own rhetoric and philosophy—before integrating such strategies. If museums cannot refer to these publicly shared policies as proof that they are practicing what they preach, they risk being viewed as insincere, self-serving, and propagandist.

The continued destruction of the archaeological record and cultural patrimony in many parts of the world is a global issue, one for which museums have been identified as being partially to blame because of direct or indirect involvement in the illicit art and antiquities market. Paradoxically, because of their vital educational role in society, museums are arguably the most powerful and passionate advocates for addressing this issue.

Appendix A: Glossary

The following definitions are provided to facilitate communication among museum staff, particularly those participating in the acquisition process. They were gleaned from a wide variety of sources, including archaeology and museum publications and policy statements, legal dictionaries, as well as definitions provided by U.S. and international legislation, treaties, and conventions. In some instances, more than one applicable definition is provided. In these cases, the definitions are labeled alphabetically and their sources are referenced accordingly in the right column. Certain definitions have been modified to meet the specific meaning intended for this book. In these cases, the definition may have been broadened to include both foreign and domestic categories. An asterisk (*) follows the definition if it has been modified from its original source.

Term	Definition	Source
Acquisition	Acquisition is the process of legally obtaining objects and their associated data for a museum through gifts, purchases, exchanges, transfers, and field collecting. (Author's note: Acquisition means the transfer of legal title and acceptance of an object or group of objects that may or may not be accessioned into the museum's collection.)	Rebecca Buck and Jean Gilmore, *The New Museum Registration Methods* (Washington, DC: AAM, 1998), 359.
Adverse possession	The attribution of legal ownership of property to a party against the holder of title under a claim of right and through actual, exclusive, open, notorious, and hostile possession of the property for the duration of the time period set by a statute of limitations.	International Foundation for Art Research (IFAR) Art Law Glossary (www.ifar.org/glossary.php)
Affidavit	1) any written document in which the signer swears under oath before a notary public or someone authorized to take oaths (like a county clerk), that the statements in the document are true, 2) in many states a declaration under penalty of perjury, which does not require the oath-taking before a notary, is the equivalent of an affidavit.	Law.com Law Dictionary
Agreement	1) A mutual understanding between two or more persons about their relative rights and duties regarding past or future performances; a manifestation of mutual assent by two or more persons. 2) The parties' actual bargain as found in their language or by implication from other circumstances, including course of dealing, usage of trade, and course of performance.	Bryan A. Garner, ed., *Black's Law Dictionary*, 8th ed. (St. Paul, MN: West Group, 2004), 74.
Antiquity	An object, especially something archaeologically, historically, or artistically valuable or interesting, that dates from a previous era. Note: This publication considers antiquities as objects over one hundred years old made by or modified by a human being. The 100 year age was determined by the definition of Archaeological Resource, as defined by the Archaeological Resources Protection Act of 1979, and the definition used by U.S. Customs.	International Foundation for Art Research (IFAR) Art Law Glossary (www.ifar.org/glossary.php)

Archaeological resource or object*	Any material remains of past human life or activities of archaeological interest. For archaeological resources originating outside the United States, the Convention on Cultural Property Implementation Act requires the material to be culturally significant and at least 250 years old. (Referred to as "Archaeological Resource" in CPIA.) For archaeological resources originating inside the United States, the Archaeological Resources Protection Act requires the material to be at least 100 years old. (Referred to as "Archaeological Object" in ARPA.) Under ARPA, archaeological objects include, but are not limited to: pottery, basketry, bottles, weapons, weapon projectiles, tools, structures or portions of structures, pit houses, rock painting, rock carvings, intaglios, graves, human skeletal materials, or any portion or piece of any of the foregoing items.	Convention on Cultural Property Implementation Act and Archaeological Resources Protection Act (http://exchanges.state.gov/heritage/culprop/laws/pdfs/2600.pdf)
Associated funerary objects	Objects that, as a part of the death rite or ceremony of a culture, are reasonably believed to have been placed with individual human remains either at the time of death or later, and both the human remains and associated funerary objects are presently in the possession or control of a federal agency or museum, except that other items exclusively made for burial purposes or to contain human remains shall be considered as associated funerary objects.	NAGPRA Glossary (www.nps.gov/nagpra/training/glossary.htm) [25 USC 3001 (3)(A)]
Bona fide purchaser	One who buys something for value without notice of another's claim to the property and without actual or constructive notice of any defects in or infirmities, claims, or equities against the seller's title; one who has in good faith paid valuable consideration for property without notice of prior adverse claims. Generally a bona fide purchaser for value is not affected by the transferor's fraud against a third party and has a superior right to the transferred property as against the transferor's creditor to the extent of the consideration that the purchaser has paid.	Bryan A. Garner, ed., *Black's Law Dictionary*, 8th ed. (St. Paul, MN: West Group, 2004), 1271.
Chance find	An archaeological object unintentionally found either above or below ground. See inadvertent discovery.	
Civil law	The prevailing system of law in continental Europe, derived from Roman law. In contrast to the traditional common law system of England and America, the basic source of law in the civil law system is organized codes rather than case-by-case judicial decisions. In the United States, Louisiana stands out as the state whose law is most heavily influenced by civil law because of its origins as a French territory.	James E. Clapp, *Webster's Legal Dictionary* (New York: Random House, 1996), 47.

Claim	1) an assertion that one is entitled to something, 2) also called claim for relief, in the federal courts and many states, an assertion of facts that, if true, would legally entitle the claimant to judgment in a civil case. A plaintiff's complaint must allege such facts or suffer dismissal for "failure to state a claim."	James E. Clapp, *Webster's Legal Dictionary* (New York: Random House, 1996), 42.
Common law	1) The legal system that evolved over many centuries in England and is the foundation of law in Great Britain and many of its former possessions, including the United States. In contrast to the civil law system of continental Europe, the basic source of common law is judicial decisions rather than codes, with judges seeking in each new case to adapt the principles worked out in previous cases to new facts and circumstances in such a way as to achieve justice, 2) Judge-made law, as distinguished from statutory law. Although large areas of earlier common law have now been codified, including criminal law and commercial law, there remain other large areas, notably torte law, contract law, and property law, that are still predominantly governed by common law rather than statutes.	James E. Clapp, *Webster's Legal Dictionary* (New York: Random House, 1996), 47
Conscious avoidance doctrine	A defendant can be held liable for his "knowledge" of fact X upon a finding that s/he was "aware of a high probability of" fact X's existence and "consciously avoided confirming that fact."	*United States v. Aina-Marshall*, 336 F.3d 167, 170 (2d Cir. 2003).
Context	The position of an archaeological find in time and space, established by measuring and assessing its associations, matrix, and provenience. The assessment includes study of what has happened to the find since it was buried in the ground.	Brian Fagan, *Archaeology*, 6th ed. (New York: Longman, 1997), 249.
Conversion	A civil wrong (tort) in which one converts another's property to his own use; in other words, "stealing." Conversion includes treating another's goods as one's own, holding onto such property which accidentally comes into the taker's hands, or purposely giving the impression that the assets belong to the taker. This gives the true owner the right to sue for his own property or the value and loss of use of it, as well recourse to law enforcement authorities, since conversion usually includes the crime of theft.	Law.com Law Dictionary (http://dictionary.law.com).

Cultural affiliation	A relationship of shared group identity which can be reasonably traced historically or prehistorically between a present-day Indian tribe or Native Hawaiian organization and an identifiable earlier group (NAGPRA, 25 U.S.C. 3001.2[3]); association of an object with the culture that produced or used it. Cultural affiliation is established when the preponderance of the evidence—based on geographical, kinship, biological, archaeological, linguistic, folklore, oral tradition, historical evidence, or other information or expert opinion—reasonably leads to such a conclusion.	NAGPRA Glossary (www.nps.gov/nagpra/training/glossary.htm) [43 CFR 10.2 (e)]
Cultural items	Associated funerary objects, unassociated funerary objects, sacred objects, and objects of cultural patrimony. [25 USC 3001 (3)]	NAGPRA Glossary (www.nps.gov/nagpra/training/glossary.htm)
Cultural property	1) Object of archaeological interest; 2) Object of ethnological interest; or 3) Fragment or part of any object referred to in (1) or (2) which was first discovered within, and is subject to export control by the State Party. [nation signing the 1970 UNESCO Convention] — syns. artifacts, antiquities, art.	Convention on Cultural Property Implementation Act
Cultural property law	A law regulating the export of cultural objects for the purpose of protecting its cultural heritage. (See Patrimony Law, Foreign Export Law, Foreign Ownership Law.)	UNIDROIT Convention on Stolen or Illegally Exported Cultural Objects, 1995.
Culturally sensitive object	A collection element that requires special handling or use restrictions due to its importance to a particular culture.	John E. Simmons, *Things Great and Small: Collections Management Policies* (Washington, DC: American Association of Museums, 2006), 169.
Culturally unidentifiable	Human remains or cultural items for which no culturally affiliated present-day Indian tribe or Native Hawaiian organization can be determined.	NAGPRA Glossary (www.nps.gov/nagpra/training/glossary.htm) [43 CFR 10.9 (d)(2)]

Deed of gift	A contract that transfers ownership of an object or objects from a donor to an institution. It should include all conditions of the gift.	AAM Registrar's Committee Glossary (www.rcaam.org)
Demand and refusal rule	A common law rule followed by New York courts providing that, in determining when a statute of limitations begins to run, the cause of action to recover stolen property from a good faith purchaser or other possessor does not accrue until the possessor refuses to return the object upon the demand of the owner.	International Foundation for Art Research (IFAR) Art Law Glossary (www.ifar.org/glossary.php)
Discovery rule	The rule that a limitations period does not begin to run until a plaintiff discovers (or reasonably should have discovered) the injury giving rise to a claim.	Bryan Garner, ed., *Black's Law Dictionary*, 8th ed. (St. Paul, MN: West Group, 2004), 499.
Documentation	A. A summary of existing museum or government agency records including inventories or catalogues, relevant studies, or other pertinent data for the limited purpose of determining the geographical origin, cultural affiliation, and basic facts surrounding the acquisition and accession of human remains and associated funerary objects.* B. Documentation of an object's provenance or provenience. Documented objects are accompanied by a credible record of origin, and at least partial information on ownership history.	A. NAGPRA Glossary (www.nps.gov/nagpra/training/glossary.htm) [43 CFR 10.9 (e)(5)] B. Marie Malaro, *A Legal Primer on Managing Museum Collections* (Washington, DC: Smithsonian, 1999), 73.
Due diligence	A. In reasonable care or attention to a matter, which is good enough to avoid a claim of negligence, or is a fair attempt (as in due diligence in a process server's attempt to locate someone). B. In determining whether the possessor exercised due diligence, regard shall be had to all the circumstances of the acquisition, including the character of the parties, the price paid, whether the possessor consulted any reasonably accessible register of stolen cultural objects, and any other relevant information and documentation which it could reasonably have obtained, and whether the possessor consulted accessible agencies or took any other step that a reasonable person would have taken in the circumstances.	A. Law.com Law Dictionary B. UNIDROIT Convention C. IFAR Art Law Glossary

	C. The diligence reasonably expected from, and ordinarily exercised by, a person who seeks to satisfy a legal requirement or to discharge an obligation. In relation to the acquisition of art, it refers to a prospective buyer's investigation and analysis of the object.	
Emergency action	Convention on Cultural Property Implementation Act action taken by the president when sites are in jeopardy from pillage, dismantling, dispersal, or fragmentation which is, or threatens to be, of crisis proportions.	Convention on Cultural Property Implementation Act
Ethnological object	Product of a tribal or non-industrial society that is important to the cultural heritage of a people because of its distinctive characteristics, comparative rarity, or its contribution to the knowledge of the origins, development, or history of that people.	Convention on Cultural Property Implementation Act
Export license	Permission, usually granted by a governmental agency, to ship cultural property out of the country.*	AAM Registrar's Committee Glossary (www.rcaam.org)
Fair market value	The value of property on the open market involving a willing buyer and a willing seller.	IFAR Art Law Glossary
Federal lands	Any land other than tribal lands that are controlled or owned by the United States government, including lands selected by but not yet conveyed to Alaska Native Corporations and groups organized pursuant to the Alaska Native Claims Settlement Act. United States "control" refers to those lands not owned by the United States but in which the United States has a legal interest sufficient to permit it to apply these regulations (43 CFR 10) without abrogating the otherwise existing legal rights of a person (see also Public Land).	NAGPRA Glossary (www.nps.gov/nagpra/training/glossary.htm) [43 CFR 10.2 (f)(1)]
Funerary object	Items that, as a part of the death rite or ceremony of a culture, are reasonably believed to have been placed intentionally with or near individual human remains at the time of death or later.	John E. Simmons, *Things Great and Small: Collections Management Policies* (Washington, DC: American Association of Museums, 2006), 170.

Good-faith purchaser	One who buys something for value without notice of another's claim to the property and without actual or constructive notice of any defects in or infirmities, claims, or equities against the seller's title; one who has in good-faith-paid valuable consideration for property without notice of prior adverse claims.	Bryan Garner, ed., *Black's Law Dictionary*, 8th ed. (St. Paul, MN: West Group, 2004), 1271.
Human remains	The physical remains of the body of a person of Native American ancestry. The term does not include remains or portions of remains that may reasonably be determined to have been freely given or naturally shed by the individual from whose body they were obtained, such as hair made into ropes or nets. For the purposes of determining cultural affiliation, human remains incorporated into a funerary object, sacred object, or object of cultural patrimony must be considered as part of that item.	NAGPRA Glossary (www.nps.gov/nagpra/training/glossary.htm) [43 CFR 10.2 (d)(1)]
Illegally excavated	Archaeological material excavated without authorization of the landowner, or contrary to applicable legislation, and without the required permits.	Author's definition
Illegal import	An item that is transferred to one country from another in violation of either the laws of the country to which the item is transferred or the laws of the item's country of origin.	IFAR Art Law Glossary
Illegally exported	Cultural objects removed from the territory of a state contrary to its law regulating the export of cultural objects for the purpose of protecting its cultural heritage.	1995 UNIDROIT Convention
Illicit	A. Illegal or improper. B. The Convention makes the "import, export or transfer of cultural property effected contrary to the provisions adopted under this Convention" illicit (Article 2). C. Examples of illicit material: unauthorized removals from authorized archaeological sites; unauthorized excavations; "appropriation" arising from war and occupation; looting of religious sanctuaries and shrines; "discovery" of objects "missing" since World War II; smuggling and in certain circumstances, illegal exports, and thefts from museums, private and public institutions, and private citizens.	A. Bryan Garner, ed., *Black's Law Dictionary*, 8th ed. (St. Paul, MN: West Group, 2004), 763. B. 1970 UNESCO Convention C. Jessica Darraby, *Art, Artifact and Architecture Law* (Eagan, MN: Thompson/West, 2006), 353.

Import	To land on, bring into, or introduce into, or attempt to land on, bring into, or introduce into any place subject to the jurisdiction of the United States, whether or not such landing, bringing, or introduction constitutes an importation within the meaning of the tariff laws of the United States. Import shipment: The shipment of an object or a group of objects into the country.	AAM Registrar's Committee Glossary (www.rcaam.org)
In rem action or proceeding	An action in which the judgment of the court determines the title to property and the rights of the parties, not merely among themselves, but also as against all persons at any time dealing with them or with the property upon which the court had adjudicated. The court's jurisdiction is based on either actual or imputed power over the property itself.	IFAR Art Law Glossary
Inadvertent discovery	The unanticipated encounter or detection of human remains, funerary objects, sacred objects, or objects of cultural patrimony found under or on the surface of federal or tribal lands pursuant to Section 3 (d) of NAGPRA. (This definition is relevant to all classes of archaeological material.*)	NAGPRA Glossary (www.nps.gov/nagpra/training/glossary.htm) [43 CFR 10.2 (g)(4)]
Indemnity	1) a duty to make good any loss, damage, or liability incurred by another, 2) the right of an injured party to claim reimbursement for its loss, damage, or liability from a person who has such a duty, 3) reimbursement or compensation for loss, damage or liability in torte; especially the right of a party who is secondarily liable for reimbursement of expenditures paid to a third party for injuries resulting from a violation of common-law duty.	Bryan Garner, ed., *Black's Law Dictionary*, 8th ed. (St. Paul, MN: West Group, 2004), 784.
Indian lands	Lands of Indian tribes, or Indian individuals, which are either held in trust by the United States or subject to a restriction against alienation imposed by the United States, except for any subsurface interests in lands not owned or controlled by an Indian tribe or an Indian individual.	Archaeological Resources Protection Act of 1979
Indian tribe	Any tribe, band, nation, or other organized group or community of Indians, including any Alaska Native village (as defined in, or established pursuant to, the Alaska Native Claims Settlement Act), which is recognized as eligible for the special programs and services provided by the United States to Indians because of their status as Indians. [25 USC 3001 (7)] This is the same as the Bureau of Indian Affairs list of federally recognized tribes, available online in PDF format. Note: There may be non-federally recognized groups which are considered stakeholders who may hold interest in collections.*	NAGPRA Glossary (www.nps.gov/nagpra/training/glossary.htm)

Intentional excavation	The planned archaeological removal of human remains, funerary objects, sacred objects, or objects of cultural patrimony found under or on the surface of federal or tribal lands pursuant to Section 3 (c) of the act. Note: This definition is relevant to all classes of archaeological material.*	NAGPRA Glossary (www.nps.gov/nagpra/training/glossary.htm) [43 CFR 10.2 (g)(3)]
Laches	A. Unreasonable delay in pursuing a right or claim, almost always an equitable one, in a way that prejudices the party against whom relief is sought. B. The defense of laches is based on equity or fairness. It essentially argues that the party seeking relief has negligently delayed taking action to the detriment of the defendant and that allowing that party to prevail would be unjust.	A. Bryan Garner, ed., *Black's Law Dictionary*, 8th ed. (St. Paul, MN: West Group, 2004), 891. B. Marie Malaro, *A Legal Primer on Managing Museum Collections* (Washington, DC: Smithsonian, 1999), 73.
Looted antiquity	Antiquities illegally and unprofessionally excavated, often with the intent of finding valuable material to sell on the market, and without regard to the item's archaeological context. Note: This term can also be used to describe "antiquities taken from the possession of individuals, institutions (such as museums or churches) or other resting places which do not harbor any archaeological interest in their link with the antiquity itself." However, these documented antiquities are more generally referred to as "stolen."	Simon R. M. Mackenzie, *Going, Going, Gone: Regulating the Market in Illicit Antiquities* (Leicester, UK: Institute of Art and Law, 2005), 6.
Minor items	A. A "Minor Item" is an object (or group of objects) valued at $5,000 or less. This term applies to material originating from within and from outside of the U.S. The $5,000 value is based upon the definition of objects covered under the Stolen Property Act, the law that has been used to successfully enforce the cultural patrimony laws of foreign nations within U.S. courts.	A. N/A

	B. An object valued under $5,000 which may be offered to the museum without acquisition history. This may be because they were illegally excavated or exported but it may equally be because none of their previous owners has ever thought it worthwhile to catalogue or record them, or to provide or keep receipts of purchase. There is also the possibility that documentary evidence of a legitimate provenance has been lost. The only satisfactory way to decide whether in individual cases it is ethically admissible to attempt to acquire such items is through the exercise of due diligence. Minor items usually share the following characteristics: may be of common types, or may be items of which multiple examples were made and have survived; are usually made of relatively inexpensive or plentifully available materials; are often (but not always) small in physical size; may lack conventional beauty or other appeal; and tend to be (but are not always) of relatively low monetary value.	B. United Kingdom Department for Culture, Media, and Property Unit, Combating Illicit Trade: Due Diligence Guidelines for Museums, Libraries and Archives on Collecting and Borrowing Cultural Material, October 2005, 10.
Negligence	The failure to exercise the standard of care that a reasonably prudent person would have exercised in a similar situation; any conduct that falls below the legal standard established to protect others against unreasonable risk of harm, except for conduct that is intentionally, wantonly, or willfully disregardful of others' rights.	Bryan Garner, ed., *Black's Law Dictionary*, 8th ed. (St. Paul, MN: West Group, 2004), 1061.
Object of cultural patrimony	An object having ongoing historical, traditional, or cultural importance central to the Native American group or culture itself, rather than property owned by an individual Native American, and which, therefore, cannot be alienated, appropriated, or conveyed by any individual regardless of whether or not the individual is a member of the Indian tribe or Native Hawaiian organization and such object shall have been considered inalienable by such Native American group at the time the object was separated from such group. Note: This essence of the above definition is internationally applicable.	NAGPRA Glossary (www.nps.gov/nagpra/training/glossary.htm) [25 USC 3001 (3)(D)]
Older collection	Refers to items originating from the United States. An "older collection" is an antiquity which has irrefutable provenance dating back to at least 1978. This term applies to material originating only from within the United States. The 1978 date is intended to predate material subject to the 1979 Archaeological Resource Protection Act (ARPA). The term is author defined and is not officially used within ARPA legislation.	n/a

Patrimony	The fundamental objects, traditions, or values that one generation or society has inherited from its ancestors.	IFAR Art Law Glossary
Patrimony law	Some countries have implemented ownership and/or export restrictions variously referred to as patrimony, umbrella, retention, or blanket laws. The objective of such laws ordinarily is to vest in the sovereign state title of objects like antiquities, historic, religious, and artistic objects—the so-called cultural patrimony of the country. The properties may be movable or immovable, privately owned or undiscovered, described generally or with specificity. In this manner, governments assert ownership although they may lack possession.	Jessica Darraby, *Art, Artifact and Architecture Law* (Eagan, MN: Thompson/West, 2006), 357.
Policy	A guideline that regulates organizational action. Policies control the conduct of people and thus the activities of the systems.	John E. Simmons, *Things Great and Small: Collections Management Policies* (Washington, DC: American Association of Museums, 2006), 172.
Possession	Having physical custody of human remains, funerary objects, sacred objects, or objects of cultural patrimony with a sufficient legal interest to lawfully treat the objects as part of its collection for purposes of these regulations. Generally, a museum or federal agency would not be considered to have possession of human remains, funerary objects, sacred objects, or objects of cultural patrimony on loan from another individual, museum, or federal agency.	NAGPRA Glossary (www.nps.gov/nagpra/training/glossary.htm) [43 CFR 10.2 (a)(3)(i)]
Preponderance of evidence	As standard of proof in civil cases, is evidence which is of greater weight or more convincing than the evidence which is offered in opposition to it; that is, evidence which as a whole shows that the fact sought to be proved is more probable than not.	NAGPRA Glossary (www.nps.gov/nagpra/training/glossary.htm)
Procedure	Specific instructions for enacting and carrying out a policy.	John E. Simmons, *Things Great and Small: Collections Management Policies* (Washington, DC: American Association of Museums, 2006), 172.

Provenance	The background and history of ownership.	John E. Simmons, *Things Great and Small: Collections Management Policies* (Washington, DC: American Association of Museums, 2006), 172.
Provenience	Defines an object in terms of the specific geographic location of origin. In scientific collections, the term "locality," meaning specific geographic point of origin, is more acceptable.	John E. Simmons, *Things Great and Small Collections Management Policies.* (Washington, DC: American Association of Museums, 2006), 172.
Public lands	Lands which are owned and administered by the United States as part of the national park system, the national wildlife refuge system, or the national forest system. All other lands that fee title to which is held by the United States, other than lands on the Outer Continental Shelf and lands which are under the jurisdiction of the Smithsonian Institution (see also Federal Land).	Archaeological Resources Protection Act of 1979
Public trust	A. A relationship in which the museum holds property that is administered for the benefit of the public. B. A trust is a fiduciary relationship whereby a party (known as a trustee) holds property that must be administered for the benefit of others (known as beneficiaries). A trustee, even though he has legal title to trust property, may not use that property for his own purposes. He may use trust assets only for the benefit of the individual or group that is the beneficiary of the trust, and in accordance with the terms of the trust. Note: A legally bound relationship under the purview of the state attorney general's office.*	A. John E. Simmons, *Things Great and Small: Collections Management Policies* (Washington, DC: American Association of Museums, 2006), 172. B. Marie Malaro, *A Legal Primer on Managing Museum Collections* (Washington, DC: Smithsonian, 1999), 73.

Repatriation	A. To return or restore the control of an object to the country of origin or rightful owner. B. In NAGPRA (25 USC 3005), the term repatriation means the transfer of physical custody of and legal interest in Native American cultural items to lineal descendants, culturally affiliated Indian tribes, and Native Hawaiian organizations. See also Disposition, Repatriate, Return, and Transfer.	A. John E. Simmons, *Things Great and Small: Collections Management Policies* (Washington, DC: American Association of Museums, 2006), 173. B. NAGPRA Glossary (www.nps.gov/nagpra/training/glossary.htm)
Replevin	A legal action in which an original owner seeks to recover possession of property wrongfully taken or retained by another party.	International Foundation for Art Research (IFAR) Art Law Glossary (www.ifar.org/glossary.php)
Repository	A facility that can provide long-term professional, systematic, and accountable curatorial services for a collection that it does not own.	John E. Simmons, *Things Great and Small: Collections Management Policies* (Washington, DC: American Association of Museums, 2006), 173.
Repository agreement	Agreement in which an institution provides long-term professional, systematic, and accountable curatorial services for a collection that belongs to another entity (e.g., a state government, federal government, or foreign government). Note: This term is most often used in the context of NAGPRA, but is also applicable to federally owned or controlled objects under the care of the museum.*	John E. Simmons, *Things Great and Small: Collections Management Policies* (Washington, DC: American Association of Museums, 2006), 173.

Right of possession	Possession obtained with the voluntary consent of an individual or group that had authority of alienation. The original acquisition of a Native American unassociated funerary object, sacred object, or object of cultural patrimony from an Indian tribe or Native Hawaiian organization with the voluntary consent of an individual or group with authority to alienate such object is deemed to give right of possession of that object, unless the phrase so defined would, as applied in Section 7(c), result in a Fifth Amendment taking by the United States as determined by the United States Claims Court pursuant to 28 U.S.C. 1491 in which event the "right of possession" shall be as provided under otherwise applicable property law. The original acquisition of Native American human remains and associated funerary objects which were excavated, exhumed, or otherwise obtained with full knowledge and consent of the next of kin or the official governing body of the appropriate culturally affiliated Indian tribe or Native Hawaiian organization is deemed to give right of possession to those remains.	NAGPRA Glossary (www.nps.gov/nagpra/training/glossary.htm) [25 USC 3001 (13)]
Risk management	The process of assessing risk and acting in such a manner, or prescribing policies and procedures, so as to avoid or minimize loss associated with such risk.	Webster's New World Law Dictionary (law.yourdictionary.com)
Sacred object	Specific ceremonial object for which is needed by traditional religious leaders for the practice of traditional religions by their present-day adherents.	NAGPRA Glossary (www.nps.gov/nagpra/training/glossary.htm)
Scienter	Latin for "having knowledge." In criminal law, it refers to knowledge by a defendant that his or her acts were illegal or his or her statements were lies and thus fraudulent.	Law.com Law Dictionary
Scientifically excavated	Procedures for field survey or excavation must meet the following minimal standards: If specimens are collected, a system for identifying and recording their proveniences must be maintained. Uncollected entities such as environmental or cultural features, depositional strata, and the like, must be fully and accurately recorded by appropriate means, and their location recorded. The methods employed in data collection must be fully and accurately described. Significant stratigraphic and/or associational relationships among artifacts, other specimens, and cultural and environmental features must also be fully and accurately recorded. All records should be intelligible to other archaeologists. If terms lacking commonly held referents are used, they should be clearly defined. Insofar as possible, the interests of other researchers should be considered. For example, upper levels of a site should be scientifically excavated and recorded whenever feasible, even if the focus of the project is on underlying levels.	Register of Professional Archaeologists, Standards of Research Performance

Statute of limitations	1) A law that bars claims after a specified period; specifically, a statute establishing a time limit for suing in a civil case, based on the date when the claim accrued (as when the injury occurred or was discovered). The purpose of such a statute is to require diligent prosecution of known claims, thereby providing finality and predictability in legal affairs and ensuring that claims will be resolved while evidence is reasonably available and fresh. 2) A statute establishing a time limit for prosecuting a crime, based on the date when the offense occurred.	Bryan Garner, ed., *Black's Law Dictionary*, 8th ed. (St. Paul, MN: West Group, 2004), 1450–1451.
Stratigraphy	Observation of the superimposed layers in an archaeological site.	Brian Fagan, *Archeology*, 6th ed. (New York: Longmans, 1997), 256.
Stolen/ stolen property	A. Stolen: A cultural object which has been unlawfully excavated or lawfully excavated but unlawfully retained shall be considered stolen, when consistent with the law of the State where the excavation took place. A cultural object that has been temporarily exported from the territory of the requesting State, for purposes such as exhibition, research or restoration, under a permit issued according to its laws regulating its export for the purpose of protecting its cultural heritage and not returned in accordance with the terms of that permit shall be deemed to have been illegally exported. B. Stolen property: Goods acquired by larceny, robbery, or theft. • Larceny: The unlawful taking and carrying away of someone else's personal property with the intent to deprive the possessor of it permanently. • Robbery: The illegal taking of property from the person or another, or in the person's presence, by violence or intimidation; aggravated larceny. • Theft: The felonious taking and removing of another's personal property with the intent of depriving the true owner of it. C. The general rule in the U.S. is that a thief cannot convey good title. Therefore, if the party transferring the object to the museum is a thief or innocently passes stolen property, the museum does not receive good title. Title probably still remains in the party who suffered the theft, and, upon demand, the object, or its value, would have to be returned to the true owner.	A. 1995 UNIDROIT Convention B. Bryan Garner, ed., *Black's Law Dictionary*, 8th ed. (St. Paul, MN: West Group, 2004), 1459. C. Marie Malaro, *A Legal Primer on Managing Museum Collections* (Washington, DC: Smithsonian, 1999), 68.

Title	A. The possession of rights of ownership of personal property. Separate rights of possession include copyright interests, trademark rights, and any specific interests that the previous owner may have reserved. B. 1) The union of all elements (as ownership, possession, and custody) constituting the legal right to control and dispose of property; the legal link between a person who owns property and the property itself. 2) Legal evidence of a person's ownership rights in property; an instrument (such as a deed) that constitutes such evidence. C. Ownership of real property or personal property, which stands against the right of anyone else to claim the property. In real property, title is evidenced by a deed, judgment of distribution from an estate, or other appropriate document recorded in the public records of the county. Title to personal property is generally shown by possession, particularly when no proof or strong evidence exists showing that the property belongs to another or that it has been stolen or known to be lost by another.	A. John E. Simmons, *Things Great and Small: Collections Management Policies* (Washington, DC: American Association of Museums, 2006), 173. B. Bryan Garner, ed., *Black's Law Dictionary*, 8th ed. (St. Paul, MN: West Group, 2004), 1522. C. Law.com Law Dictionary
Tribal land	All lands within the exterior boundaries of any Indian reservation; all dependent Indian communities; any lands administered for the benefit of Native Hawaiians pursuant to the Hawaiian Homes Commission Act of 1920, and Section 4 of Public Law 86-3. [25 USC 3001 (15)] All lands which are within the exterior boundaries of any Indian reservation including, but not limited to, allotments held in trust or subject to a restriction on alienation by the United States; or comprise dependent Indian communities as recognized pursuant to 18 U.S.C. 1151; or are administered for the benefit of Native Hawaiians pursuant to the Hawaiian Homes Commission Act of 1920 and Section 4 of the Hawaiian Statehood Admission Act (Pub.L. 86-3; 73 Stat. 6). Actions authorized or required under these regulations [43 CFR 10] will not apply to tribal lands to the extent that any action would result in a taking of property without compensation within the meaning of the Fifth Amendment of the United States Constitution. [43 CFR 10.2 (f)(2)]	NAGPRA Glossary (www.nps.gov/nagpra/training/glossary.htm)

Unassociated funerary object	Objects that, as a part of the death rite or ceremony of a culture, are reasonably believed to have been placed with individual human remains either at the time of death or later, where the remains are not in the possession or control of the federal agency or museum and the objects can be identified by a preponderance of the evidence as related to specific individuals or families or to known human remains or, by a preponderance of the evidence, as having been removed from a specific burial site of an individual culturally affiliated with a particular Indian tribe. Those funerary objects for which the human remains with which they were placed intentionally are not in the possession or control of a museum or federal agency.	NAGPRA Glossary (www.nps.gov/nagpra/training/glossary.htm) [25 USC 3001 (3)(B)] [43 CFR 10.2 (d)(2)(ii)]
Undocumented objects	A. Objects in the collections that lack any useful documentation as to how they were acquired. B. Collections that cannot be determined to have been collected, exported, and imported in full compliance with the laws and regulations of the country or countries of origin, of the federal government of the United States, and of individual states within the United States and International treaties, even when the U.S. is not a signatory. Such provision includes materials collected under circumstances that would support or encourage irresponsible damage to/or destruction of biota, collecting sites, cultural monuments, or human burial places. This policy constitutes adherence to all existing laws and regulations and to the guidelines of professional societies.	A. AAM Registrar's Committee Glossary (www.rcaam.org) B. American Institute of Archaeology Code of Ethics
Uniform Commercial Code	A uniform law that governs commercial transactions, including sales of goods, secured transactions, and negotiable instruments. The code has been adopted in some form by every state in the United States.	Bryan Garner, ed., *Black's Law Dictionary*, 8th ed. (St. Paul, MN: West Group, 2004), 1565.
Unscientifically excavated	Procedures for field survey or excavation which do NOT meet the minimal standards set forth above under the definition of *Scientifically Excavated*.	Register of Professional Archaeologists, Standards of Research Performance
Warrant	1) to guarantee the security of (realty or personality, or a person), 2) to give warrantee of (title) to a (person) < the seller warrants the property's title >, 3) to promise or guarantee < warrant payment >.	Bryan Garner, ed., *Black's Law Dictionary*, 8th ed. (St. Paul, MN: West Group, 2004), 1616.

Appendix B: Sample Acquisition Guidelines and Questionnaire

Thank you for your interest in donating to X Museum. Please review the following acquisition guidelines. If you feel that your potential donation meets these guidelines, please complete the attached Acquisition Questionnaire and submit with photos of the objects for review.

Acquisition Guidelines

Please review the following guidelines for museum acquisitions:

1. The object supports the museum's mission and public trust responsibilities, and consistent with and relevant to the stated purpose, scope, and activities of the museum. The object is valuable for the purposes of education and programming. The object meets a specific need, or fills a specific gap in the existing collection, and this need can be articulated as a collecting priority by the curatorial staff.
2. The object warrants the use of the museum's financial, personnel, and physical resources to ensure its proper storage, protection, care, documentation, and accessibility, in keeping with professionally accepted standards. No item(s) will be considered for acquisition if future care and preservation needs exceed the museum's resources. Donations that include financial support for long-term storage and preservation are encouraged.
3. The object's title is transferred free and clear, without restrictions. All acquisitions are to be outright and unconditional. All donations to the museum's collections are irrevocable upon the formal and physical transfer to the museum. All legal instruments of conveyance and warranty of title, signed by the donor/seller/agent setting forth an adequate description of the items involved and the precise conditions of the transfer shall accompany all acquisitions.
4. The object poses no or negligible risk to the safety of museum staff, visitors, or to other objects within the collection; or if the condition of object is compromised, its treatment and storage needs are balanced by its curatorial value.

5. Donors must provide verifiable record of authenticity and provenance for all proposed donations. The quality and completeness of the documentation accompanying an object is a decisive factor in considering its potential acquisition. Objects with incomplete provenance will be given preference if there is evidence that suggests there is strong certainty that the object's context, origin, and history may be discerned through further research. Exceptions of this type should be made only for items only after due diligence has provided assurance that the object was not illegally excavated or exported.
6. The museum will make every effort to ascertain that items offered are not stolen, wrongfully converted, or acquired under false pretences. The museum is bound by U.S. and international antiquities and endangered species laws. If the museum discovers that it has acquired item (s) in violation of U.S. or international legislation, the museum shall seek to return the item(s) to the legal owner or shall seek to determine the proper means of disposition through recognized authorities. The museum wishes to demonstrate its continued good-faith efforts to preserve the global, cultural, and natural heritage and maintain an open dialogue that enables the museum to work collaboratively and cooperatively with the international community toward their common goals. In this spirit, the museum may contact authorities from countries of origin or descendant communities if there is doubt about the legality of a potential acquisition.
7. The acquisition is consistent with the museum's desire to promote the protection and preservation of natural and cultural resources and discourage illicit trade in these items. The acquisition does not encourage unscientific excavations of archaeological materials. Considerations for the acquisition of unscientifically excavated or documented archaeological materials may include, but are not strictly limited to, prevention of random disposal that would distort the archaeological record, preservation of significant archaeological information, and promotion of pubic education about the value of archaeological investigations *in situ*.
8. All acquisitions by gift or bequest to the museum will remain in the possession of the museum for as long as they retain their physical integrity and authenticity and remain useful for the purposes of the museum. Curatorial decisions may result in objects being deemed more appropriate for use in our education department or to be offered for sale to benefit the museum.

To assist the Collections Committee in making an informed decision about accepting the artifacts you may wish to donate, we ask that you fill out the following Donor Questionnaire. Please complete the information to the best of your ability. Provide additional sheets as needed. You may wish to complete a separate questionnaire for each proposed donation.

Once you return the questionnaire with photograph(s) of the object, the registrar will circulate the information among the members of the Collections Committee who will make an initial determination of whether the artifact complements our collecting mission and whether we have the resources to properly care for the items. If the committee decides to consider the object for acquisition, you will be contacted to make available the item and original documentation for committee review. The museum is unable to acquire an object until after due diligence research has been satisfactorily undertaken. This process may take up to ninety days to complete.

The museum will make every effort to ascertain that items offered are not stolen, wrongfully converted, or acquired under false pretences. The museum is bound by international and domestic antiquities laws and internal university regulations. Foreign antiquities must have documentation indicating that they were not exported from their country of origin after November 11, 1970 (**or other date** determined by museum's legal counsel and governing authority) in violation of international cultural property laws. Proof of such documentation will be needed before the acquisition review process can be initiated.

Please note that federal law prevents the museum from providing identification services or appraisal values for donated items. Donors are responsible for appraisals of value. Please contact the regional branch of the Appraisers Association of America or the American Society of Appraisers directly. The museum is in no way affiliated with these organizations.

Donations are fully tax deductible within IRS guidelines. Please consult your tax advisor.

Thank you.

X Museum

Acquisition Questionnaire

Date: ____

Name: ____

Address: ____

____

Phone Number(s): ___________________________________

Email Address: _____________________________________

Are you the legal owner of the artifact?
YES _____ NO _____ UNKNOWN _____

Are you the owner's authorized agent for the purpose of passing title?
YES _____ NO _____ UNKNOWN _____

Comments: ____

____

Are you aware of any other potential claims of ownership?
YES _____ NO _____ UNKNOWN _____

Comments: ____

____

Number of objects you wish to donate: __________________

Appraised value of object(s) you wish to donate: ___________

____

Brief description of object(s) including materials, measurements, and condition: ____

____

____

____

____

If from outside the United States, list the object's country of origin. If known, list any intermediate countries where the object was transported. Indicate dates of exportation and importation, if known.

If from inside the United States, list the state(s) where the item originated, and, if known, list the owner of land where the object originated. If unknown, please indicate whether the item may have originated from federally or tribally owned or controlled land.

When and how did the objects come into the possession of the current owner or agent? Who were the objects acquired from?

What is the object's provenance (history of ownership)? Please provide as much specific information as possible, including names and contact information for prior owners and dates of transfer.

What kinds of documentation are available? (The following types of documents might provide acceptable evidence of provenance: will/inventory, photographic evidence, diaries, correspondence, auction or exhibition catalogues, bill of sale/sales receipt, excavation field notes, excavation permits, insurance record, publication in a reputable source, export license from country of origin, import/export documents from intermediate country, and/or U.S. customs documents, professional appraisals.) Please note below what documentation is available and if they are original or copies:

Does the object incorporate any fish and wildlife components?
YES ____ NO ____ UNKNOWN ____

If yes, please indicate which permits or other documentation can be provided to demonstrate that the object was collected, transported, exported, imported, acquired, transferred, and possessed in compliance with all U.S. and foreign laws: ____________________

____

____

Has the artifact been treated with preservative chemicals, such as moth balls or insecticide? YES ____ NO ____ UNKNOWN ____

If yes, please explain: ____________________________

____

Other comments regarding your artifacts or the acquisition review process: ____________________________

____

____

The museum accepts a stewardship responsibility for donated objects, which creates a financial obligation in perpetuity. Will a financial contribution be available to assist the museum with the care of these objects?

YES ____ NO ____

Thank you again for considering the X Museum for your donation. Should you have any questions, please feel free to contact **registrar's name** at **phone number** or **email address**.

Mail your completed questionnaire and photos of the objects you wish to donate to:

Mailing address

Appendix C: Examples of Basic Criteria for Acquisition of Domestic Cultural Material

Material Restricted and Documentation Required to Meet Sample Basic Criteria for Acquisition of Domestic Cultural Material

Table C.1:

No.	Criterion	Material Restricted	Documentation Required
1.	Require permits and other documentation for archaeological resources or cultural items originating from federally owned or controlled lands after 1905.	1a. Objects of antiquity from archaeological sites, historic or prehistoric ruins, or monuments from federally owned and controlled lands between 1906 and 1978 (covered under the Antiquities Act). 1b. Archaeological resources excavated from federally owned and controlled lands after 1979 (covered under the ARPA), defined as: any material remain of past human life or activities that are of archaeological interest, including, but not limited to: pottery, basketry,	1a. Federally issued Antiquities Act granted by the secretaries of the interior, agriculture, or army to institutions. Record of title given to institution responsible for excavation, or transfer of title from that institution to current donor. Memorandum of Agreement (MOA) with federal agency outlining curation standards in line with Federal Regulation 36 CFR 79.

Continued

Table C.1: *continued*

No.	Criterion	Material Restricted	Documentation Required
		bottles, weapons, weapon projectiles, tools, structures or portions of structures, pit houses, rock paintings, rock carvings, intaglios, graves, human skeletal materials, or any portion or piece of any of the foregoing items that are at least 100 years of age.	1b. Federally issued ARPA permit required. (Note: Title is retained by federal government.) MOA with federal agency outlining curation standards in line with Federal Regulation 36 CFR 79.
		1c. Native American cultural items, including human remains, associated or unassociated funerary objects, sacred objects, and objects of cultural patrimony, which show a relationship of lineal descent or cultural affiliation to a federally recognized tribe, that were excavated after 1990 on federally owned or controlled lands. (Cultural items covered under NAGPRA are defined below under Criteria #4.)	1c. Federally issued ARPA permit required. Evidence of tribal consultation, including written plan of action and/or notice of intended disposition. Depository agreement with tribal government. (Note: Title is retained by the federal or tribal government.)
2.	Require permits and other documentation for archaeological resource or cultural items originating from tribally owned or controlled lands after 1978.	2a. Archaeological resources over 100 years old as defined above under "b" in Criterion #1, which were excavated from tribally owned or controlled lands after 1978 (covered under the ARPA). 2b. Native American cultural items, including human remains, associated or unassociated funerary objects, sacred objects, and objects of cultural patrimony, which show a relationship of lineal descent or cultural affiliation to a federally recognized tribe, that were excavated after 1990 on tribally owned or controlled lands. (Cultural items covered under NAGPRA are defined below under Criterion #4.)	2a. Federally issued ARPA permit required. (Note: Title is retained by federal government.) MOA with federal agency outlining curation standards in line with Federal Regulation 36 CFR 79. 2b. Federally issued ARPA permit required. Evidence of tribal consultation, including written plan of action and/or notice of intended disposition. Depository agreement with tribal government. (Note: Title is retained by the federal or tribal government.)

Table C.1: *continued*

No.	Criterion	Material Restricted	Documentation Required
3.	Have reasonable assurance the object was not illegally excavated from lands controlled by any state or municipal statutes (particularly those relating to burial sites or restricting the sale, transport, or possession of archaeological material) after the effective date of applicable statutes.	Ensure the circumstances of acquisition in no way indicate the material was acquired in violation of any state statute, such as those concerning theft, conversion, or trespass. Special attention should be given to material that may have been excavated from a burial or cemetery on public or private property or archaeological material from publicly owned land. Laws may also restrict material originating from a locally or state-recognized historic private property, or a property that has a preservation restriction or easement placed on it, although these restrictions are atypical.	• Documented findings from search of one or more of sources of information on state laws, or state historic preservation office website. Specific attention should be given to material resulting from burial sites, cemeteries, and state or municipally owned properties. • Depending on the specifics of the case (date of find, etc.), either search online and document findings or request the donor sign a statement indicating that, to the best of his or her knowledge, the excavation and transfer of the item was lawful. • The state archaeologist should be consulted with questions.
4.	Have reasonable assurance that any cultural items as defined by NAGPRA (human remains, associated or unassociated funerary objects, sacred objects, or objects of cultural patrimony),	The NAGPRA future applicability rule is triggered by the nature of the cultural material; the date and origin of collection are not factors. a. Human remains: The physical remains of the body of a person of Native American ancestry. The term does not include remains or portions of remains that may reasonably be determined to have been freely given or naturally shed by the individual from whose body they were obtained, such as hair made into ropes or nets. For the purposes of determining cultural	Documentation showing the item to be held with right of possession. Right of possession is defined as: Possession obtained with the voluntary consent of an individual or group that had authority of alienation. The original acquisition of a Native American unassociated funerary object, sacred object, or object of cultural patrimony

Continued

Table C.1: *continued*

No.	Criterion	Material Restricted	Documentation Required
	is being transferred with clear right of possession.	affiliation, human remains incorporated into a funerary object, sacred object, or object of cultural patrimony must be considered as part of that item. [43 CFR 10.2 (d)(1)] b. Associated funerary objects: Objects that, as a part of the death rite or ceremony of a culture, are reasonably believed to have been placed with individual human remains either at the time of death or later, and both the human remains and associated funerary objects are presently in the possession or control of a federal agency or museum, except that other items exclusively made for burial purposes or to contain human remains shall be considered as associated funerary objects. [25 USC 3001 (3)(A)] c. Unassociated funerary objects: Objects that, as a part of the death rite or ceremony of a culture, are reasonably believed to have been placed with individual human remains either at the time of death or later, where the remains are not in the possession or control of the federal agency or museum and the objects can be identified by a preponderance of the evidence as related to specific individuals or families or to known human remains or, by a preponderance of the evidence, as having been removed from a specific burial site of an individual culturally affiliated with a particular Indian tribe. [25 USC 3001 (3)(B)]	from an Indian tribe, or Native Hawaiian organization with the voluntary consent of an individual or group with authority to alienate such object is deemed to give right of possession of that object…. The original acquisition of Native American human remains and associated funerary objects which were excavated, exhumed, or otherwise obtained with full knowledge and consent of the next of kin or the official governing body of the appropriate culturally affiliated Indian tribe or Native Hawaiian organization is deemed to give right of possession to those remains. [25 USC 3001 (13)] With the exception of human remains, other NAGPRA-defined cultural items (funerary, sacred, and patrimonial) may be acquired unless they originated from federal or tribal lands after 1990. However, it is likely that such items will be repatriated. In such cases, the museum may wish to serve as a temporary depository to facilitate repatriation, so long as doing so does not provide

Table C.1: *continued*

No.	Criterion	Material Restricted	Documentation Required
		d. Those funerary objects for which the human remains with which they were placed intentionally are not in the possession or control of a museum or federal agency. [43 CFR 10.2 (d)(2)(ii)] e. Sacred objects: Specific ceremonial objects that are needed by traditional Native American religious leaders for the practice of traditional Native American religions by their present-day adherents. [25 USC 3001 (3)(C)] f. Object of cultural patrimony: An object having ongoing historical, traditional, or cultural importance central to the Native American group or culture itself, rather than property owned by an individual Native American, and that, therefore, cannot be alienated, appropriated, or conveyed by any individual regardless of whether or not the individual is a member of the Indian tribe or Native Hawaiian organization and such object shall have been considered inalienable by such Native American group at the time the object was separated from such group. [25 USC 3001 (3)(D)]	material incentive to current looting and it does not violate state law. It is advisable to consult with tribal groups before doing so. The acquisition of human remains of indigenous origin is not recommended for procedural and ethical reasons. The NAGPRA rule on culturally unidentifiable/unaffiliated human remains requires museums to follow a procedure that may result in repatriation to tribal groups living in the area where the human remains were found. The museum may wish to develop a policy that enables it to take custody of such material to facilitate repatriation. This safe-harbor provision may be utilized in the event that the donor intends to discard material otherwise.
5.	Require evidence the owner of the private property where the archaeological material originated	While this book does not recommend that a museum acquire an object lacking complete provenance information, a museum may choose to identify possible scenarios where exceptions may be made. Legal counsel should be consulted when establishing these exceptions.	• Archaeological material reportedly collected from private lands as part of a professional archaeological investigation should be accompanied by permits, stamps, and verification forms, in addition to

Continued

Table C.1: *continued*

No.	Criterion	Material Restricted	Documentation Required
	permitted the excavation, removal, and transfer of the object and renounced further claims to the object, with possible exceptions as defined by the museum.	Below are two examples of exceptional circumstances a museum may incorporate into their basic criteria for acquisition if doing so is in line with their institutional and ethical considerations, and upon approval of the museum's legal counsel and governing board: • A "minor item" is an object (or group of objects) valued at $5,000 or less. This term applies to material originating from within and from outside the United States. The $5,000 value is based on the definition of objects covered under the Stolen Property Act. • An "older collection" is an antiquity with documented provenance dating back to at least 1978. The 1978 date is intended to predate material subject to the 1979 Archaeological Resource Protection Act.	field notes and documentation. • Exceptions made for material meeting the "minor item" or "older collection" definition must be accompanied by a credible account of provenance from a trustworthy donor; and, as a result of due diligence, there is no indication of the item's illegal or questionable nature, including objects that appear "freshly excavated, from a 'hot' area, or a 'hot' category of item."[1] Furthermore, the museum may accept the object so long as no federal, state, or local laws are identified that prohibit transfer. A signed affidavit warranting the item's provenance should be required. Ideally, this document should indemnify the museum by stating the museum will not be held responsible for any expenses incurred by ownership claims made by a tribal group, or other party.

Appendix D: Examples of Basic Criteria for Acquisition of Foreign Cultural Material

Material Restricted and Documentation Required to Meet Sample Basic Criteria for Acquisition of Foreign Cultural Material

Table D.1:

No.	Criterion	Material Restricted	Documentation Required
1.	Require evidence the object is not covered under the regulation of importation of pre-Columbian monumental or architectural sculpture or murals.	Pre-Columbian monumental or architectural sculpture or murals from Bolivia, Belize (British Honduras), Columbia, Costa Rica, Dominican Republic, Ecuador, El Salvador, Guatemala, Honduras, Mexico, Panama, Peru, or Venezuela exported after June 1, 1973.	• A certificate, issued by the government of the country of origin of such sculpture or mural, in a form acceptable to the secretary of the treasury, certifying that such exportation was not in violation of the laws of that country; or • Satisfactory evidence that such sculpture or mural was exported from the country of origin on or before June 1, 1973; or • Satisfactory evidence that such sculpture or mural is not an article subject to the Pre-Columbian Monumental Act and regulations.[1]

Continued

Table D.1: ***continued***

No.	Criterion	Material Restricted	Documentation Required
2.	Required evidence that the object is not designated as restricted under the Convention on Cultural Property Implementation Act.	As of November 2010, designated cultural property from the following countries was restricted: Bolivia, Cambodia, China, Columbia, Cyprus, El Salvador, Belize, Guatemala, Honduras, Iraq, Italy, Mali, Nicaragua, and Peru. (Canada's Bilateral Agreement was applicable between April 22, 1997 and April 9, 2002.)	• A certificate or other documentation issued by the government of the country of origin certifying the exportation was not in violation of laws of that country; or • Satisfactory evidence that the designated material was exported from the state party not less than ten years before the date of entry and neither the person for whose account the material was imported (or any related party) contracted for or acquired an interest in the material more than one year before the date of entry; or • Satisfactory evidence that the designated material was exported from the state party on or before the date that the material was designated under 19 USC §2604.[2]
3.	Have reasonable assurance the object was not reported stolen by a foreign country.	• Items inventoried by a museum of similar institution or objects that may be traced to official excavation site in the country of origin. (CPIA limits restriction to countries who are signatory to the UNESCO Convention.) • Pre-Columbian property from Mexico, Peru, Ecuador, and Guatemala stolen from federal, state, or municipal governments or their instrumentalities, covered under U.S. treaties and executive agreements. • Other known items reported stolen.	• Printed results of database for stolen art (Trace.com for most items, and certificate from Art-Loss Register for unique and/or valuable items). • Documented investigation of website(s) from the likely country or countries of origin, the UNESCO website, and a general Internet search for key words describing the item.

Table D.1: ***continued***

No.	Criterion	Material Restricted	Documentation Required
4.	Have reasonable assurance the item is not subject to U.S. customs import restrictions or sanctions.	Nearly all property from Iraq, Cuba, Iran, Sudan, and Burma, as well as material from the Balkans, Belarus, Côte d'Ivoire, Democratic Republic of Congo, Iraq, Lebanon, North Korea, Somalia, Syria, and Zimbabwe.	• Documentation required by U.S. customs and/ or website, or customs documents showing the item was imported prior to effective date of the sanction, or is not subject to said sanction.
5.	Require evidence the object was not exported after November 17, 1970 in violation of export or ownership laws of the country of origin and/or the country where it was last legally owned.	Items restricted by foreign law.	• Documented findings from search of IFAR and UNESCO databases and other sources of information on foreign cultural property laws. • Associated documentation that provides concrete and irrefutable proof of the object's legal exportation after the museum's established cutoff date (foreign export license from country of origin as well as any other intermediate country).
6.	Have reasonable assurance the item was not exported before November 17, 1970 in violation of foreign law, with possible exceptions as defined by the museum.	While this book does not recommend that a museum acquire an object lacking complete provenance and provenience information, a museum may choose to identify possible scenarios where exceptions may be made. Legal counsel should be consulted when establishing these exceptions, and these should be approved by the governing board. Possible exception may be granted for items lacking export documentation, so long as the export did violate a foreign law clearly deeding ownership	• Documented findings from search of IFAR and UNESCO databases and other sources. • If the law clearly deeds ownership of the material to the country of origin, then the item must not be acquired unless the item is determined to be a minor item and is accompanied by a notarized affidavit warranting the provenance of the object and releasing the museum from harm. • If the law does not clearly deeds ownership of the material to the country of origin and merely prohibits export, then the item may be acquired,

Continued

Table D.1: ***continued***

No.	Criterion	Material Restricted	Documentation Required
		of the item at the time of export. Determination requires legal counsel. Below are examples of exceptional circumstances a museum may incorporate into their basic criteria for acquisition if doing so is in line with their institutional and ethical considerations, and upon approval of the museum's legal counsel and governing board: • Possible exceptions include "minor items" and "adequately publicized works," so long as doing so does not conflict with state law. • Items valued over $5,000, require notification of foreign country representative.	although a signed affidavit warranting provenance is advisable. The museum may also only want to make this exception for minor objects, and/or after contacting country of origin representatives. • Any material acquired in contravention of foreign law must be accompanied by a credible account of provenance from a trustworthy donor, and, as a result of due diligence, there is no indication of the item's illegal or questionable nature, including objects that appear "freshly excavated, from a 'hot' area, or a 'hot' category of item."[3] Furthermore, the museum must ensure that no federal, state, or local laws are identified that prohibit transfer. A signed affidavit warranting the item's provenance should be required. Ideally, this document should indemnify the museum by stating the museum will not be held responsible for any expenses incurred by ownership claims made by a tribal group or other party. Other required documentation may include export permits; independent appraisal for valuations of under $5,000, documented analysis of foreign property law (including statement by legal counsel), and state law search documentation.

Table D.1: ***continued***

No.	Criterion	Material Restricted	Documentation Required
7.	Require evidence the object was legally imported into the United States after November 17, 1970. Have reasonable assurance the item was legally imported prior to this date, with possible exceptions as defined by museum.	Possible exceptions include "minor items," so long as doing so does not conflict with state or federal law.	Request donor signs an affidavit and warranty of title, and request dealer, if purchased, to sign an indemnity agreement.

Appendix E: Foreign Cultural Property Restrictions

The evaluation of the legal status for objects from outside the United States requires museums to consider many factors. The process is outlined in greater detail in Chapter 7, but Table E.2, Restrictions Governing the Cultural Property of Foreign Countries, was created as a resource to aid in the review process. As the legal rules governing the acquisition of foreign property are in flux, the user must confirm that new developments have not superseded material listed on this table. To the best of my knowledge, the material below is current as of November 28, 2010. Table E.1 provides an overview of the information included in Table E.2.

Table E.1: Guide to Format and Codes Used in Table E.2

Column Number/ Title	Overview of Covered Material	Guide to Codes and Sources
Column 1: Country	Lists countries that are: • impacted by any U.S. legislation, treaties, executive agreements, or customs embargoes; • have accessible cultural property laws, with the dates of those laws; • have accepted or ratified the 1970 UNESCO Convention, with the date of that action; or • were identified as a source country for particular types of items subject to illicit trade, or have historical resources in danger of destruction.[1]	

Continued

Table E.1: *continued*

Column Number/ Title	Overview of Covered Material	Guide to Codes and Sources
Column 2: Legislation/ Treaties/Sanctions	Lists countries covered by: • the Cultural Property Implementation Act (CPIA)[2]; • the Pre-Columbian Monumental, Architectural Sculpture or Murals Act; • customs sanctions; and • U.S. treaties and executive agreements.	• CPIA-BA: CPIA bilateral agreements or memorandums of understanding • CPIA-EA: CPIA Emergency Agreements • Pre-Columbian: Pre-Columbian Monumental, Architectural Sculpture or Murals Act[3] • Sanctions: U.S. customs sanctions[4] • U.S./Mexico: Treaty of Cooperation between the United States of America and the United Mexican States Providing for the Recovery and Return of Stolen Archaeological, Historical, and Cultural Properties[5] • U.S./Peru: Agreement between the United States and Republic of Peru for Recovery and Return of Stolen Archaeological, Historical, and Cultural Properties[6] • U.S./Guatemala: Agreement between the United States and the Republic of Guatemala for Recovery, and Return of Stolen Archaeological, Historical, and Cultural Properties[7] • U.S./Ecuador: Agreement between the United States and Ecuador for Recovery and Return of Stolen Archaeological, Historical, and Cultural Properties[8]

Table E.1: ***continued***

Column Number/ Title	Overview of Covered Material	Guide to Codes and Sources
Column 3: Cultural Property Law Source	Countries that have cultural property laws listed in the four commonly known resources. Museum staff should check both online sources to ensure that the country or origin or intermediate country has not enacted cultural property laws subsequent to the publication of this table.	Sources: • I: International Foundation for Art Research. International Cultural Property/ Ownership & Export Legislation (ICPOEL)[9] • U: The UNESCO cultural heritage laws database[10] • H: *Handbook of National Regulations Concerning the Export of Cultural Property*[11] • C: Collection of Legislative Texts Concerning the Protection of Movable Cultural Property[12]
Column 4: Dates of Enforcement (or Update) of Foreign Cultural Property Laws	Effective or updated date of foreign cultural property laws.	
Column 5: UNESCO Status	Countries that have accepted or ratified the 1970 UNESCO Convention on the Means of Prohibiting, and Preventing the Illicit Import, Export, and Transfer of Ownership of Cultural Property.	This information is included for museums choosing to only honor cultural property laws only for signatories of the convention.[13]
Column 6: Red Flag	Origin of cultural goods most affected by looting and theft. Museums should proceed with great caution when considering the acquisition of cultural property originating from these countries, particularly those property types, or from specific regions, that are listed as threatened.	R: ICOM Red List[14] D: UNESCO World Heritage in Danger List[15]

Table E.2: Restrictions Governing Cultural Property of Foreign Countries

Country	Legislation/ Treaties/ Sanctions	Cultural Property Law Source	Dates of Enforcement (or Update) of Foreign Cultural Property Laws	UNESCO Status	Red Flag
Afghanistan		I, H	1958, 2004	Acceptance—2005	R, D
Albania		I, U, H	1971, 1994, 2003	Acceptance—2002	
Algeria		I, U, H	1967, 1969, 1998	Ratification—1974	
Andorra		U	2003		
Angola		U, H	1976	Ratification—1991	
Argentina		I, U, H	1913, 1921, 1940, 1996, 1997, 2003, 2004	Ratification—1993	
Armenia		U	2004	Notification of succession—1993	
Australia		I, U, H	1976, 1978, 1986, 1987, 2001, 2002, 2005	Acceptance—1989	
Austria		I, H	1978, 1985, 1999		
Azerbaijan		U	1996	Ratification—1999	
Bahamas				Ratification—1997	
Bahrain		I, H	1970, 1995		
Bangladesh		I, H	1968	Ratification—1987	
Barbados		H	1981	Acceptance—2002	
Belarus	Sanctions	U	1992	Ratification—1988	

Table E.2: *continued*

Country	Legislation/ Treaties/ Sanctions	Cultural Property Law Source	Dates of Enforcement (or Update) of Foreign Cultural Property Laws	UNESCO Status	Red Flag
Belgium		I, U, H	1931, 1996, 1999, 2002, 2003, 2004, 2008	Ratification—2009	
Belize		I, U, C, H	1971, 1972, 1990, 2000	Ratification—1990	R, D
Benin		U, H	1968		
Bhutan		I, U	2005	Ratification—2002	
Bolivia	CPIA-EA (1989–1996); CPIA-BA (2001–2011); Pre-Columbian	I, H	1927, 1961, 1976, 1978, 1997, 2004	Ratification—1976	
Bosnia and Herzegovina		I, U	1995, 2001, 2002, 2003	Notification of succession—1993	
Botswana		I, W, H	1970, 2004		
Brazil		C, H	1937	Ratification—1973	
British Honduras	Pre-Columbian				
Brunei Darussalam		I	1967		
Bulgaria		I, H	1969, 2004, 2005, 2006	Ratification—1971	
Burkina Faso		I, U, H	1985, 1987, 1999	Ratification—1987	R
Myanmar	Sanctions	H	1957		

Continued

Table E.2: *continued*

Country	Legislation/ Treaties/ Sanctions	Cultural Property Law Source	Dates of Enforcement (or Update) of Foreign Cultural Property Laws	UNESCO Status	Red Flag
Burundi		H	1939		
Byelorussian Soviet Socialist Republics		H	1976		
Cambodia	CPIA-EA (1999–2002); CPIA-BA (2003–2008)	I	1996	Ratification—1972	R
Cameroon		U, H	1963	Ratification—1972	R
Canada	CPIA-EA (1997–2002)	I, U, H	1977, 1985	Acceptance—1978	
Central African Republic		H	1956	Ratification—1972	D
Chad		U, H	1960	Ratification—2008	R
Chile		I, U, H	1966, 1969, 1970, 1976, 1990, 1993, 1997, 2005, 2010		D
China	CPIA-BA (2009–2014)	I, U, H	1982, 1989, 1991, 2001, 2002, 2003, 2007	Acceptance—1989	
Colombia	CPIA-BA (2006–2011)	I, H	1959, 1991, 1997, 2008	Acceptance—1988	R, D
Comoros		U, H	1956		
Congo (the Democratic Republic of Libian Arab Lamahiriya)		U, H	1956	Ratification—1974	D
Costa Rica	Pre-Columbian	I, U, H	1923, 1938, 1981, 1982, 1989, 1995, 1999	Ratification—1996	R

Table E.2: *continued*

Country	Legislation/ Treaties/ Sanctions	Cultural Property Law Source	Dates of Enforcement (or Update) of Foreign Cultural Property Laws	UNESCO Status	Red Flag
Croatia		I	1999	Notification of succession—1992	
Cuba	Sanctions	I, U, C, H	1976, 1977, 1979, 1983, 1987, 1989, 1992, 1994, 1995, 1996, 1997, 1999	Ratification—1980	
Cyprus	CPIA-BA: (2002–2006/Arch); (1999–2003/Ethno); (2007–2011/Ethn & Arch)	I, C, H, U	1935, 1964, 1996, 2001	Ratification—1979	
Czechoslovakia		H	1958		
Czech Republic		I	1958, 1987, 1994, 2000	Notification of succession—1992	
Democratic Kampuchea		H	1925		
Democratic Yemen		H	1970		
Denmark		I, H	1986, 1987, 2001	Ratification—2003	
Dominican Republic		C, H, U	1968	Ratification—1973	
Ecuador	Pre-Columbian; U.S./Ecuador Treaty	I, U, C, H	1978, 1979, 1984, 2001	Acceptance—1971	R, D
Egypt		I, U, C, H	1983	Acceptance—1973	D

Continued

Table E.2: *continued*

Country	Legislation/ Treaties/ Sanctions	Cultural Property Law Source	Dates of Enforcement (or Update) of Foreign Cultural Property Laws	UNESCO Status	Red Flag
El Salvador	CPIA-EA (1987–1995); CPIA-BA (1995–2010); Pre-Columbian	I, H	1983, 1993	Ratification—1978	R
Equatorial Guinea				Ratification—2010	
Estonia		I, U, H	1998, 1999, 2002, 2003	Ratification—1995	
Ethiopia		I, U, H	1969, 2000		D
Fiji		I, H	1940, 1945, 1986		
Finland		I, U, H	1963, 1999	Ratification—1999	
France		I, U, H	1913, 1992, 2000, 2004	Ratification—1997	
Gabon		U, H	1956	Acceptance—2003	
Gambia		U, H	1974		
Georgia		I, U	1996, 1999	Notification of succession—1992	D
Germany		I	1955, 2001, 2007	Ratification—2007	
Germany (Democratic Republic of)		H	1953		
Germany (Federal Republic of)		H	1955		
Ghana		I, U, H	1969, 1973		R

Table E.2: *continued*

Country	Legislation/ Treaties/ Sanctions	Cultural Property Law Source	Dates of Enforcement (or Update) of Foreign Cultural Property Laws	UNESCO Status	Red Flag
Greece		I, U, C, H	1932, 2002, 2008	Ratification—1981	
Grenada				Acceptance—1992	
Guatemala	CPIA-EA (1991–1996); CPIA-BA (1997–2011); Pre-Columbian	I, U, H	1947, 1965, 1966, 1985, 1993, 1997	Ratification—1985	R
Guinea		U, H	1956	Ratification—1979	D
Guyana		H	1972		
Haiti		C, H	1940	Ratification—2010	R
Holy See		H	See Italy		
Honduras	CPIA-BA (2004–2009); Pre-Columbian	I, C, H	1982, 1984, 1997	Ratification—1979	R
Hungary		I, C, H, U	1963, 1997, 2001	Ratification—1978	
Iceland		H	1969	Ratification—2004	
India		I, U, H	1904, 1972, 1976, 1979	Ratification—1977	D
Indonesia		I, H	1931, 1992, 1993		
Iran (Islamic Republic of)	Sanctions	C, H	1930	Acceptance—1975	D
Iraq	Sanctions	I, H	1936, 1974, 1975, 2002	Acceptance—1973	R, D
Ireland		I, U, C, H	1930, 1945, 1954, 1987, 1994, 1997, 2004		

Continued

Table E.2: *continued*

Country	Legislation/ Treaties/ Sanctions	Cultural Property Law Source	Dates of Enforcement (or Update) of Foreign Cultural Property Laws	UNESCO Status	Red Flag
Israel		I, H	1978, 1989		
Italy	CPIA-BA (2001–2011)	I, U, H	1939, 1975, 1998, 2004	Ratification—1978	
Ivory Coast (Côte d'Ivoire)	Sanctions	I, U, H	1987, 1999	Ratification—1990	R, D
Jamaica		H	1985		
Japan		I, H, U	1950, 1961, 2002	Acceptance—2002	
Jordan		U, H	1976	Ratification—1974	
Kazakhstan		U	1996		
Kenya		U, C, H	1983		
Korea (Democratic People's Republic of)	Sanctions			Ratification—1983	
Korea (Republic of Korea)		I, U, C, H	1982, 1983, 2002, 2004	Acceptance—1983	
Kuwait		U, H	1960	Acceptance—1972	
Kyrgyzstan		U	1992	Acceptance—1995	
Lao People's Democratic Republic		H	1982		
Latvia		U	1993		

Table E.2: *continued*

Country	Legislation/ Treaties/ Sanctions	Cultural Property Law Source	Dates of Enforcement (or Update) of Foreign Cultural Property Laws	UNESCO Status	Red Flag
Lebanon	Sanctions	H	1933	Ratification—1992	
Lesotho		C, H, U	1967		
Liberia	Sanctions	U	2002		
Libyan Arab Jamahiriya		H	1968	Ratification—1973	
Lichtenstein		I, H	1977		
Lithuania		I, U	1994, 1996, 2004, 2005	Ratification—1998	
Luxembourg		U, H	1966		
Macedonia (the former Yugoslav Republic of)		I, U	2004, 2005, 2007	Notification of succession—1997	
Madagascar		U, H	1973	Ratification—1989	D
Malawi		I, U, H	1965, 1990		
Malaysia (none), West Malaysia (1954), Sabah (1976), and Sarawak (1977)		H	1954–1977		
Mali	CPIA-EA (1993–1996); CPIA-BA (1997–2011)	I, U, H	1973, 1985, 1987	Ratification—1987	R
Malta		H	1925		

Continued

Table E.2: *continued*

Country	Legislation/ Treaties/ Sanctions	Cultural Property Law Source	Dates of Enforcement (or Update) of Foreign Cultural Property Laws	UNESCO Status	Red Flag
Mauritania		U, H	1972	Ratification—1977	
Mauritius		U, H	1944	Acceptance—1978	
Mexico	Pre-Columbian; U.S./Mexico Treaty	I, U, C, H	1928, 1972, 1975, 1986, 1993, 2004	Acceptance—1972	R
Moldova (Republic of)		U	1993	Ratification—2007	
Monaco		U	1928		
Mongolia		H	1970	Acceptance—1991	
Montenegro		W	1991		
Morocco		C, H, U	2002	Ratification—2003	
Nepal		U, H	1956	Ratification—1976	
Netherlands		I, H	1984, 1985, 1988, 2002	Acceptance—2009	
New Zealand		I, H	1975	Acceptance—2007	
Nicaragua	CPIA-BA	I, C, H	1980, 1982, 1983	Ratification—1977	R
Niger		U, H	1956	Ratification—1972	R, D
Nigeria		U, H	1979	Ratification—1972	R
Norway		I, H	1978, 1979, 2000, 2001	Ratification—2007	
Oman				Acceptance—1978	

Table E.2: *continued*

Country	Legislation/ Treaties/ Sanctions	Cultural Property Law Source	Dates of Enforcement (or Update) of Foreign Cultural Property Laws	UNESCO Status	Red Flag
Pakistan		I, H	1975, 1979, 1992	Ratification—1981	D
Panama	Pre-Columbian	I, H	1982, 2003, 2004	Acceptance—1973	R
Papua New Guinea		H	1965		
Paraguay		H	1943	Ratification—2004	
Peru	CPIA-EA (1990–1996); CPIA-BA (1997–2011); Pre-Columbian; U.S./Peru Treaty	I, H	1929, 1936, 1958, 1984, 1985, 1993, 2004, 2006	Acceptance—1979	R, D
Philippines		I, U, H	1974, 2009, 2010		D
Poland		H	1962	Ratification—1974	
Portugal		U, H	1985	Ratification—1985	
Qatar		C, H	1980	Acceptance—1977	
Romania		U, H	1974	Acceptance—1993	
Russian Federation		U	1993	Ratification—1988	
Rwanda		U, H	1939	Ratification—2001	
Saint Vincent and the Grenadines		H	1976		
Samoa		H	1954		

Continued

Table E.2: *continued*

Country	Legislation/ Treaties/ Sanctions	Cultural Property Law Source	Dates of Enforcement (or Update) of Foreign Cultural Property Laws	UNESCO Status	Red Flag
San Marino		U	1995		
Saudi Arabia		U, H	1972	Acceptance—1976	
Senegal		H	1971	Ratification—1984	D
Serbia		U	1994		D
Seychelles		U, H	1980		
Sierra Leone		H	1947		
Singapore		I	1970, 1993, 2004		
Slovakia		I, U	1998, 2001, 2002	Notification of succession—1993	
Slovenia		I, U	1999, 2003	Notification of succession—1992	
Somalia	Sanctions				
South Africa		I, U	1999, 2002	Acceptance—2003	
Spain		I, H	1985, 1986, 1995	Ratification—1986	
Sri Lanka		H	1940	Acceptance—1981	
Sudan	Sanctions	I, U, H	1952		
Suriname		H	1952		
Swaziland		U, H	1972		

Table E.2: *continued*

Country	Legislation/ Treaties/ Sanctions	Cultural Property Law Source	Dates of Enforcement (or Update) of Foreign Cultural Property Laws	UNESCO Status	Red Flag
Sweden		I, U, H	1960, 1985, 1986, 1988, 2000, 2002	Ratification—2003	
Switzerland		I, U, H	1963, 1990, 2003, 2005, 2007	Acceptance—2003	
Syrian Arab Republic (Syria)	Sanctions	U, H	1963	Acceptance—1975	
Tajikistan		U	1997	Ratification—1992	
Tanzania (United Republic of)		C, U	1979	Ratification—1977	D
Thailand		I, H	1961, 1992		
Togo		U, H	1956		
Tonga		I, H	1969, 1970		
Tunisia		U, C, H	1886	Acceptance—1975	
Turkey		I, U, H	1983, 1987, 2004	Ratification—1981	
Uganda		I, U, H	1967, 1968	Ratification—1988	D
Ukraine		W	1992		
Ukrainian Soviet Socialist Republic		H	1976		

Continued

Table E.2: *continued*

Country	Legislation/ Treaties/ Sanctions	Cultural Property Law Source	Dates of Enforcement (or Update) of Foreign Cultural Property Laws	UNESCO Status	Red Flag
Union of Soviet Socialist Republics		H	1976		
United Arab Emirates		H	1970		
United Kingdom of Great Britain and Northern Ireland		I, U, H	1939, 1996, 2002, 2003, 2004, 2007	Acceptance—2002	
United States of America		I, H	1948, 1979, 1994, 1999, 2004, 2007	Acceptance—1983	D
Uruguay		C, H, U	1971	Ratification—1996	
Uzbekistan		I, U	1998, 2001	Ratification—1996	
Vanuatu		I	1965, 2008		
Venezuela (Bolivarian Republic of)	Pre-Columbian	I, U, H	1945, 1992, 1993, 1994, 1999, 2005, 2009	Acceptance—2005	D
Viet Nam		I, U, H	1945	Ratification—2005	
Yemen		H	1972		D
Yugoslavia		H	1967		
Zaire		H	1971		
Zambia		I, U, H	1948, 1966, 1989	Ratification—1985	
Zimbabwe	Sanctions	I, U, H	1972, 2001	Acceptance—2006	

Appendix F: Additional Resources

Codes of Ethics and Position Papers

- American Anthropological Association (AAA) Code of Ethics
  <http://www.aaanet.org/committees/ethics/ethcode.htm>

- American Association of Museums (AAM) Code of Ethics for Museums
  <http://www.aam-us.org/museumresources/ethics/coe.cfm>

- American Association of Museums (AAM) Standards Regarding Archaeological Material and Ancient Art
  <http://www.aam-us.org/museumresources/ethics/upload/Standards%20Regarding%20Archaeological%20Material%20and%20Ancient%20Art.pdf>

- Archaeological Institute of America (AIA) Code of Ethics
  <http://www.archaeological.org/pdfs/AIA_Code_of_EthicsA5S.pdf>

- Association of Art Museum Directors, Art Museums and the International Exchange of Cultural Artifacts, Position Paper
  <http://www.aamd.org/papers/documents/CulturalProperty_000.pdf>

- Association of Art Museum Directors Code of Ethics
  <http://www.aamd.org/about/#Code>

- Association of Art Museum Directors, New Report on Acquisition of Archaeological Materials and Ancient Art
  <http://aamd.org/newsroom/documents/2008ReportAndRelease.pdf>

- Association of Art Museum Directors, Report of the AAMD Subcommittee on the Acquisition and Stewardship of Sacred Objects
  <http://www.aamd.org/papers/documents/SacredObjectsReleaseandGuidelinesCombined8.9.06-dated.pdf>

- College Art Association (CAA) Resolution Concerning the Acquisition of Cultural Properties Originating in Foreign Countries
<http://www.collegeart.org/guidelines/cultpropres.html>

- International Council of Museums (ICOM) Code of Ethics for Museums
<http://icom.museum/ethics.html#begin>

- International Council on Monuments and Sites (ICOMOS) Ethical Commitment Statement
<http://www.international.icomos.org/ethic_eng.htm>

- UNESCO International Code of Ethics for Dealers in Cultural Property
<http://portal.unesco.org/culture/en/ev.php-URL_ID=13095&URL_DO=DO_TOPIC&URL_SECTION=201.html>

Resources for Cultural Property Originating within the United States

Legislation

1. Antiquities Act of 1906 [16 U.S.C. 431-433 (1906)] (Antiquities Act)
<http://www.cr.nps.gov/local-law/anti1906.htm>

2. Archaeological Resources Protection Act [16 U.S.C. §§ 470aa-470mm (1979)] (ARPA)
<http://uscode.house.gov/download/pls/16C1B.txt>

   ARPA Implementing Regulation (43 CFR Part 7)
<http://www.access.gpo.gov/nara/cfr/waisidx_02/43cfr7_02.html>

3. Native American Graves Protection and Repatriation Act [Public Law 101-601, 25 U.S.C. §§ 3001-3013 (1990)] (NAGPRA)
< uscode.house.gov/download/pls/25C32.txt>
National NAGPRA website: <http://www.cr.nps.gov/nagpra/>
Regulations: <http://www.cr.nps.gov/nagpra/MANDATES/43_CFR_10_10-1-03.pdf>
Future Applicability Rule: <http://www.cr.nps.gov/nagpra/MANDATES/Future_Applicability_Final_Rule.htm>

4. National Stolen Property Act [18 U.S.C. § 2314-2315 (1948)] (NSPA)
<http://exchanges.state.gov/heritage/culprop/index/pdfs/nspa.pdf>

5. Curation of Federally Owned and Administered Archaeological Collections (36 CFR 79)
<http://www.cr.nps.gov/archeology/tools/36cfr79.htm>

6. Local and state laws governing historical properties and archaeological resources:

   - The National Conference of State Legislatures State Historic Preservation Legislation Database, 1999

<http://204.131.235.67/programs/arts/statehist.htm>

- The Compilation of State Repatriation, Reburial, and Grave Protection Laws, July 1997
  <http://www.ibsgwatch.imagedjinn.com/learn/lawsstate.htm>

- Carol L. Carnett, A Survey of State Statutes Protecting Archeological Resources, Archeological Assistance Study, Number 3, National Trust for Historic Preservation and the U.S. Department of the Interior National Park Service, Cultural Resources, Archeological Assistance Division, August 1995.

- When in doubt, it is advisable to contact the state or tribal preservation officers or state archaeologists for additional information.

  - National Conference of State Historic Preservation Officers
    <http://www.ncshpo.org/find/index.htm>

  - National Association of Tribal Historic Preservation Officers
    <http://www.nathpo.org/map.html>

  - The National Association of State Archaeologists
    <http://www.uiowa.edu/~osa/nasa/>

  - LexisNexis Martindale-Hubbell, Martindale-Hubbell Law Digest: U.S. States, U.S. Federal, U.S. Copyright, Patent, Trademark (New Providence, NJ: LexisNexis, 2006).

Additional Resources

- Arrowheads database of State Burial Laws provides a periodically updated listing.
  <http://arrowheads.com/index.php/component/content/category/34>

- The Indian Burials and Sacred Grounds Watch website provides a list of federal and state-protected Indian burial grounds and mounds.
  <http://www.ibsgwatch.imagedjinn.com/learn/learn2.htm>

- The Nation Register Information System Database
  <http://www.nr.nps.gov/nrloc1.htm>

- The National Atlas of the United States of America facilitates in determining the likelihood of material originating from federal or tribal lands. This interactive map is available online at: <http://nationalatlas.gov/mapmaker>

- National Park Service Archaeology Program website
  <http://www.cr.nps.gov/archeology/tools/laws/ARPA.htm>

- National Trust for Historic Preservation
  <http://www.preservationnation.org/resources/legal-resources/understanding-preservation-law/federal-law/>

Resources for Cultural Property Originating from Outside the United States

United States Legislation

1. UNESCO Convention on the Means of Prohibiting and Preventing the Illicit Import, Export, and Transfer of Ownership of Cultural Property (1970) (UNESCO Convention) <http://portal.unesco.org/la/convention.asp?KO=13039&language=E&order=alpha>
2. Convention on Cultural Property Implementation Act [19 U.S.C §§ 2601-2613, regulations: 19 CFR §§ 12.104-12.104i. (1982)] (CPIA)
   A list of current and expired CPIA agreements can be found at <http://exchanges.state.gov/heritage/culprop/listactions.html>

   An interactive chart that may be organized by country or chronologically may be found at <http://exchanges.state.gov/culprop/chart2.html>

   An image database of restricted objects with links to image collection for each country is available at: <http://exchanges.state.gov/heritage/culprop/databas1.html>
3. Regulation of Importation of Pre-Columbian Monumental or Architectural Sculpture or Murals [19 U.S.C §§2091-2095 and the implementing regulations at 19 CFR §§12.105-12.109 (1972)] (Pre-Columbian Act)
   <http://exchanges.state.gov/heritage/culprop/index/pdfs/92-587.pdf>
4. National Stolen Property Act [18 U.S.C. § 2314 (1948)] (NSPA)
   <http://exchanges.state.gov/heritage/culprop/index/pdfs/nspa.pdf>

U.S. Customs Restrictions and Sanctions

- U.S. Customs and Border Protection. Informed Compliance publications
  <http://www.cbp.gov/xp/cgov/trade/legal/informed_compliance_pubs>

- U.S. Department of the Treasury, Sanctions Programs
  <http://www.treasury.gov/resource-center/sanctions/Programs/Pages/Programs.aspx>

Foreign Cultural Property Laws

- International Foundation for Art Research. International Cultural Property/Ownership & Export Legislation (ICPOEL)
  <http://www.ifar.org/icpoel.php>
  Database considered the most accessible and comprehensive listing of foreign cultural property laws, covering both export and ownership. This site is updated as new information is provided to IFAR. Provides summaries of legislation and complete text (provided in original language and with English translation, when applicable). Relevant case law is discussed and tied to relevant legislation. Links to relevant international conventions and bilateral agreements, as well as contact information for government officials who may be contacted with questions, are provided.

- The UNESCO Cultural Heritage Laws Database
<http://www.unesco.org/culture/natlaws/index.php?&lng=en>
A number of the cultural property laws are provided only in the language of the country of origin. The effective date of the legislation is not always discernable. This site is updated as UNESCO is informed of applicable laws and should be consulted prior to acquiring foreign cultural material.

- UNESCO, The Collection of Legislative Texts Concerning the Protection of Movable Cultural Property (UNESCO: 1985–1988)
<http://www.unesco.org/library/>
(Search for: "Collection of Legislative Texts Concerning the Protection of Movable Cultural Property," followed by the country in question.) Compilation of separate booklets listing legislation for twenty-five countries. Each booklet contains a summary page that serves as an index to the legislation.

Additional Resources

- When in doubt, it is advisable to contact a representative of the country of origin at the embassy in the United States or in the country itself. The site provides information on each of the embassies in Washington, DC, with links to web-based resources where available.
<http://www.embassy.org/embassies/>

- The United States Customs and Border Protection, Department of Homeland Security publication, What Every Member of the Trade Community Should Know about Works of Art, Collector's Pieces, Antiques, and Other Cultural Property, May 2006.
<http://www.cbp.gov/linkhandler/cgov/trade/legal/informed_compliance_pubs/icp061.ctt/icp061.pdf>

- The United States Customs and Border Protection
<http://www.cbp.gov/xp/cgov/trade/>

- The United States Customs and Border Protection: Entry Summary (CBP Form 7501), June 2009.
<http://forms.cbp.gov/pdf/CBP_Form_7501.pdf>

- World Customs Organization
<http://www.wcoomd.org/home.htm>

- United Kingdom Department for Culture, Media, and Sport. Combating Illicit Trade: Due Diligence Guidelines for Museums, Libraries, and Archives on Collecting and Borrowing Cultural Material (London: Crown Copyright, October 2005).
<http://www.culture.gov.uk/images/publications/Combating_Illicit_Trade05.pdf>

- United Nations Educational, Scientific, and Cultural Organization, Culture Division
<http://portal.unesco.org/culture/en/ev.php-URL_ID=34603&URL_DO=DO_TOPIC&URL_SECTION=201.html>

- International Council of Museums (ICOM)
  <http://icom.museum/>
  Under resources, hosts online information. Under fighting the illicit traffic in cultural property, has information about conventions, legislations, police and custom organizations, information on stolen objects, and articles on the issue of spoliation of Jewish cultural property during World War II.

- The ICOM Red List
  <http://icom.museum/what-we-do/programmes/fighting-illicit-traffic/red-list.html>

- International Council on Monuments and Sites (ICOMOS)
  <http://www.icomos.org>

- International Foundation for Art Research (IFAR)
  <http://www.ifar.org>

- Lawyers Committee for Cultural Heritage Preservation (LCCHP)
  <http://www.culturalheritagelaw.org>

- Saving Antiquities for Everyone
  <http://www.savingantiquities.org>

RESOURCES ON STOLEN ART AND CULTURAL PROPERTY

- AAMD Registry of New Acquisitions of Archaeological Material and Works of Ancient Art
  <http://aamdobjectregistry.org/Antiquities>

- The International Foundation for Art Research (IFAR) (A not-for-profit educational and research organization dedicated to integrity in the visual arts. IFAR offers impartial and authoritative information on authenticity, ownership, theft, and other artistic, legal, and ethical issues concerning art objects.)
  <http://www.ifar.org/index.htm>

- The Art Loss Register (a private database of stolen art and antiquities includes works of art looted during World War II, which are identified separately.)
  <http://www.artloss.com>

- Interpol Cultural Property Program
  <http://www.interpol.int/Public/WorkOfArt/Default.asp>

- FBI Art Theft Program
  <http://www.fbi.gov/about-us/investigate/vc_majorthefts/arttheft>

- Museum Security Network
  <http://www.savingantiquities.org>

- Trace (service for locating and retrieving stolen art, antiques and collectables, English)
  <http://www.trace.com>

General Resources

- International Foundation for Art Research, Inc.
  <http://www.ifar.org>
  IFAR is a not-for-profit educational and research organization that provides information on authenticity, ownership, theft, and other artistic, legal, and ethical issues concerning art objects. Website provides a variety of useful educational services including: the International Cultural Property Ownership and Export Legislation (ICPOEL) and Case Law and Statutes (CLS) databases; a glossary of terms; links to professional guidelines; useful recommendations for collectors; and a guide to provenance. IFAR also publishes the *IFAR Journal* and other publications, sponsors events, and provides an art authentication service.

- The Registrars Committee of the American Association of Museums
  <http://www.rcaam.org/>
  Website for members of RC-AAM. Provides useful information for museum registrars including glossary, references, and publications. Provides listserve forum for information exchange.

Resources for Cultural Property Types Outside the Scope of This Book

Material Originating from Underwater Sites and Shipwrecks

- 2001 UNESCO Convention on the Protection of the Underwater Cultural Heritage

- U.S. Abandoned Shipwreck Act (Pub.L. 100-298; 43 U.S.C. 2101-2106) of 1998

Nazi-Era Material

- American Association of Museums (AAM), Guidelines Concerning the Unlawful Appropriation of Objects during the Nazi Era
  <http://www.aam-us.org/museumresources/ethics/upload/ethicsguidelines_naziera.pdf>

- Association of Art Museum Directors (AAMD), Task Force on the Spoliation of Art during the Nazi/WWII Era (1933–1945)
  <http://www.aamd.org/papers/documents/Nazi-lootedart_clean_06_2007.pdf>

Resources for WWII-Era Provenance Research

- Art Loss Register
  <http://www.artloss.com/>

- The Central Registry of Information on Looted Cultural Property, 1933–1945
  <http://www.lootedart.com/>

- Commission for Looted Art in Europe (CLAE)
  <http://www.lootedartcommission.com/>

- The International Foundation for Art Research provides additional links to research resources
<http://www.ifar.org/provenance_guide.php>

Endangered Species and Items Incorporating Wildlife

- The Lacey Act
- Convention on International Trade in Endangered Species of Wild Fauna and Flora
- Endangered Species Act; Marine Mammal Protection Act
- Migratory Bird Treaty Act
- Bald and Golden Eagle Protection Act
- The Wild Exotic Bird Conservation Act
- Asian Elephant Conservation Act
- African Elephant Conservation Act
- The Antarctic Conservation Act

Summaries of and links to the following federal statutes are provided at Michigan State University College of Law Animal Legal and Historical Center.
<http://www.animallaw.info/statutes/stfedset.htm>

Human Remains

- Theresa L. Leming, "Dead Bodies," *American Jurisprudence: A Modern Comprehensive Text Statement of American Law*, vol. 22A, §3 (St. Paul, MN: West Group, 2003).

Notes

Preface

1. United Kingdom Department for Culture, Media and Sport, *Combating Illicit Trade: Due Diligence Guidelines for Museums, Libraries and Archives on Collecting and Borrowing Cultural Material*, London: Crown Copyright, Oct. 2005. 7 Feb. 2011 <http://www.culture.gov.uk/images/publications/Combating_Illicit_Trade05.pdf> (Hereafter: United Kingdom, Guidelines).
2. Paul Roberts, "Barriers or Bridges? Museums and Acquisitions." In *Who Owns Objects? The Ethics and Politics of Collecting Cultural Artefacts, Proceedings for the First St Cross—All Souls Seminar Series and Workshop, Oxford, October–December 2004*, eds. E. Robson, L. Treadwell, and C. Gosden (Oxford: Oxbow Books, 2006), 47–59.
3. Marie Malaro, *A Legal Primer on Managing Museum Collections* (Washington, DC: Smithsonian, 1999).

Chapter 1

1. Jason Felch and Ralph Frammolino, "Several Museums May Possess Looted Art; Italian Prosecutors Use Photos Seized from a Convicted Trafficker of Stolen Antiquities to Identify Dozens of Suspect Object," *Los Angeles Times*, 8 Nov. 2005, A16.
2. Edward Wyatt, "Museum Workers Are Called Complicit," nytimes.com, 26 Jan. 2008.
3. Hugh Eakin, "Italy Focuses on a Princeton Curator in an Antiquities Investigation," nytimes.com, 2 June 2010.
4. "Fed Agents Raid California Museums for Looted Artifacts," *Fox News*, 24 Jan. 2008. 3 Feb. 2010 <http://www.foxnews.com/story/0,2933,325405,00.html#ixzz17G6v77p4>.

5. Jason Felch, "Raids Suggest a Deeper Network of Looted Art," *Los Angeles Times*, 25 Jan. 2008. 3 Feb. 2010 <http://www.latimes.com/news/loca/la-me-museums25jan25,0,101198.story>.
6. Stephen Litt, "Cleveland Museum of Art Will Return Tainted Antiquities to Italy Wednesday," Cleveland.com, 21 Apr. 2009. 3 Dec. 2010. <http://www.cleveland.com/arts/index.ssf/2009/04/cleveland_museum_of_art_will_r.html>.
7. Francis P. McManamon and Susan D. Morton, "Reducing the Illegal Trafficking in Antiquities." In *Cultural Management in Contemporary Society: Perspectives on Managing and Presenting the Past*, eds. Francis P. McManamon and Alf Harton (London and New York: Routledge, 2000), 249. McManamon and Morton propose three ways for individuals or organizations to fight back against the destruction of archaeological sites from looting and trafficking:

> They can demonstrate through their own behavior, standards, and explicit ethical statements that looting and trafficking are the wrong way to treat archaeological resources. They can work to enforce existing laws against these activities more effectively and cooperate with law enforcement authorities in this endeavor. Finally, they can explain to members of the general public the true values for commemoration, education and knowledge that archaeological sites have if properly investigated and preserved.

The authors' thesis is, in part, based on these recommendations. However, they also wish to provide strategies for protecting museums and museum staff in both a legal and public relations sense, in addition to protecting our global cultural heritage.

Chapter 2

1. Exceptions include material originating from underwater sites and shipwrecks, human remains, Nazi-era material, endangered species and items including wildlife, and other issues effecting the general quality or completeness of title, including copyright issues and other restrictions, unresolved claims on bequeathed material, etc. Resources for finding out more about this material are provided in Appendix F.
2. Barbara Hoffman, *Art and Cultural Heritage: Law, Policy, and Practice* (New York: Cambridge University Press, 2006), 90.
3. Bryan Garner, ed. *Black's Law Dictionary*, 8th ed. (St. Paul, MN: West Group, 2004), 1373.
4. David A. Thomas, "Adverse Possession: Acquiring Title to Stolen Personal Property," *Probate & Property* 10 (Mar./Apr. 1996), 12.

5. Thomas, 12.
6. Steven A. Bibas, "The Case against Statutes of Limitation for Stolen Art," *Yale Law Journal* 103 (1993–1994), 2442.
7. Marie Malaro, *A Legal Primer on Managing Museum Collections* (Washington, DC: Smithsonian, 1999), 82.
8. Malaro, 73.
9. See Richard B. Cunningham, ed., *Archaeology, Relics and the Law*, 2nd ed. (Durham, NC: Carolina Academic Press, 2005), 135–136.

Common law typically holds that material found above ground, such as material that has surfaced due to erosion, lost, or abandoned, goes to the finder of the object. Title to abandoned or lost property is given to the finder, who receives a "right to possess the property against the entire world but the rightful owner regardless of the place of finding" (Cunningham, 135). However, finders who are convicted of trespassing may be required to relinquish title to the owner of the property on which it was found. An exception is made for mislaid property, "that which the owner has intentionally set down in a place where he can again resort to it, and then forgets where he put it" (see note re exception below); property must be handed over to the landowner where the object was found because they are in a better position to return it to the rightful owner who may return to the place where the object was mislaid. The landowner does not obtain title immediately, rather they serve as a bailee responsible for safeguarding mislaid items. [Note: An exception is made for mislaid property, "that which the owner has intentionally set down in a place where he can again resort to it, and then forgets where he put it"; this property must be handed over to the landowner where the object was found because they are in a better position to return it to the rightful owner who may return to the place where the object was mislaid. The landowner does not obtain title immediately, rather they serve as a bailee responsible for safeguarding mislaid items (Cunningham, 135).]

Under the common law of finds, any material found embedded in or firmly affixed to the ground is granted to the owner of the land in which the object was embedded. Many antiquities offered to museums are archaeological materials, which are generally considered "embedded property." As ownership of such property rests with the owner of the land, evidence is required that the landowner permitted the excavation and transferred title and all associated property rights, the landowner is the current possessor/donor of the object, or sufficient time has passed that enabled the current possessor to perfect title through adverse possession.

An exception to this rule may be made for "treasure trove," "a category exclusively for gold or silver in coin, plate, bullion, and sometimes its paper equivalents, found concealed in the earth or in a house or other private place" (Cunningham, 135). Treasure trove carries with it the thought of antiquity (i.e., that the treasure has been concealed for so long as to indicate that the owner is probably dead or unknown). Historically, the treasure trove doctrine in the United States recognized possession to be with the finder rather than the landowner. However, since the 1950s, state and federal courts have decided against the treasure trove doctrine, believing that the "finder's keepers" rule invites trespassers to dig at will on another person's property (Cunningham, 136).

10. Hoffman, 90.
11. U.S. Department of the Interior, National Park Service, Cultural Resources Programs, *Federal Historic Preservation Laws* (Washington, DC, 1993), 45.
12. Martin E. McAllister, "Looting and Vandalism of Archaeological Resources on Federal and Indian Lands in the United States." In *Protecting the Past*, eds. G. Smith and J. Ehrehard, 3 Aug. 2000, 3; National Park Service Southeast Archeological Center, 3 Feb. 2011 <http://www.cr.nps.gov/seac/protecting/html/3c-mcallister.htm>.
13. Archaeological Resources Protection Act [16 U.S.C 470ee(c)]. See also *U.S. v. Gerber*, 999 F2d 1112 (7th Cir. 1993), affirming the conviction. Gerber and others were criminally charged under ARPA for removing archeological resources from private land and transporting the items across state lines. The defendants questioned the validity of 16 U.S.C 470ee(c).
14. Antiquities Act of 1906 [16 U.S.C. §§ 432].
15. National Park Service, Archaeology Program, 18 Jan. 2007. 22 Oct. 2010 <http://www.cr.nps.gov/archeology/tools/laws/ARPA.htm>.
16. Archaeological Resources Protection Act [16 U.S.C. § 470ee].
17. Department of the Interior, Office of the Secretary, "Curation of Federally-Owned and Administered Archaeological Collections," 36 CFR 79 *Federal Register* 55 (12 Sept. 1990): 37670.
18. Native American Graves Protection and Repatriation Act (NAGPRA) [18 U.S.C. § 1170].
19. Final Rule, Native American Graves Protection and Repatriation Act Regulations—Disposition of Culturally Unidentifiable Human Remains, 75 Federal Register 12377, 15 Mar. 2010, effective 14 May 2010 <http://edocket.access.gpo.gov/2010/2010-5283.htm>.
20. Department of the Interior, Office of the Secretary, 43 CFR 10.13 *Federal Register* 72 (21 Mar. 2007): 54; 13184, 17 Oct. 2007 (43 CFR 10.13) <http://www.gpo.gov/fdsys/pkg/CFR-2010-title43-vol1/xml/CFR-2010-title43-vol1-sec10-13.xml >.
21. Carol L. Carnett, *A Survey of State Statutes Protecting Archeological Resources* (Washington, DC: National Trust for Historic Preservation;

U.S. Department of the Interior, National Park Service, Cultural Resources Division, Archeological Assistance Division, Aug. 1995), 1.

22. John M. Fowler, "The Legal Structure for the Protection of Archaeological Resources." In *Protecting the Past*, eds. G. Smith and J. Ehrehard (Atlanta: National Park Service, Southeast Archeological Center), 3 Aug. 2000. 14 Aug. 2010. <http://www.cr.nps.gov/seac/protecting/word/2a-fowler.doc>.
23. Fowler, 3.
24. Cunningham, 599.
25. Cunningham, 599–600.
26. Fowler, 4.
27. *United States v. Gerber*, 999 F. 2d 1112, 1114 (7th Cir. 1993). *U. S. v. Gerber* applied ARPA to private property in the United States, as actions were contrary to Indiana's laws of trespass and conversion.
28. Treaty of Cooperation between the United States of America and the United Mexican States Providing for the Recovery and Return of Stolen Archaeological, Historical, and Cultural Properties, 17 July 1970 (22 U.S.T. 494, Article 1).
29. Agreement between the United States and Republic of Peru for Recovery and Return of Stolen Archaeological, Historical and Cultural Properties, 15 Sept. 1981 (T.I.A.S. No. 10136, 33 U.S.T. 1608).
30. Agreement between the United States and Ecuador for Recovery and Return of Stolen Archaeological, Historical and Cultural Properties, 17 Nov. 1983. 14 Jan. 1987 (T.I.A.S. No. 11075).
31. Agreement between the United States and the Republic of Guatemala for Recovery and Return of Stolen Archaeological, Historical and Cultural Properties, 21 May 1984. 12 Aug. 1984 (T.I.A.S. No. 11077).
32. U.S. Department of the Treasury Office of Foreign Assets Control Sanctions Programs, 24 Nov. 2010 <http://www.ustreas.gov/offices/enforcement/ofac/programs/index.shtml>.
33. United States Customs and Border Protection, Department of Homeland Security, What Every Member of the Trade Community Should Know about Works of Art, Collector's Pieces, Antiques, and Other Cultural Property, 15 May 2006. 9 Jan. 2011 <http://www.cbp.gov> (Hereafter: United States Customs).
34. U.S. State Department, Bureau of Educational and Cultural Affairs, Chart of Current and Expired Import Restrictions under the Convention on Cultural Property Implementation Act, 17 Nov. 2010 <http://exchanges.state.gov/heritage/culprop/chart2.pdf>.
35. United Nations Educational, Scientific, and Cultural Organization, Convention on the Means of Prohibiting and Preventing the Illicit

Import, Export, and Transfer of Ownership of Cultural Property (Paris, 14 Nov. 1970), 5 Dec. 2010 <http://www.unesco.org/culture/laws/1970/html_ eng/page2.shtml>.

36. United States Customs, 14.
37. Albert E. Elsen, John Heny Merryman, and Stephen K. Urice, *Law, Ethics and the Visual Arts*, 5th ed. (The Netherlands: Klewer Law International B.V., 2007), 278.
38. The Second Federal Court District includes New York, Connecticut, and Vermont.
39. The Fifth Federal Court District includes Texas, Louisiana, and Mississippi.
40. The Ninth Federal Court District includes California, Nevada, Arizona, Washington, Oregon, Alaska, Idaho, Montana, Hawaii, Guam, and the Northern Mariana Islands.
41. Ildiko DeAngelis, "How Much Provenance Is Enough? Post-Schultz Guidelines for Art Museum Acquisition of Archaeological Materials and Ancient Art." In *Art and Cultural Heritage: Law, Policies and Practices*, ed. Barbara Hoffman (Cambridge, UK: Cambridge University Press, 2005), 400.
42. *U.S. v. Hollinshead*, 495 F.2d 1154 (9th Cir. 1974).
43. *U.S. v. McClain*, 545 F.2nd 988 (5th Cir. 1977) and *U.S. v. McClain*, 593 F. 2nd 658 (5th Cir. 1979), cert. denied, 444 U.S. 918.
44. Malaro, 108.
45. *Govt. of Peru v. Johnson*, 720 F. Supp. 810 (S.D. Cal 1989) aff'd, 933 F. 2d 1013 (9th Cir. 1991).
46. DeAngelis, 400.
47. *U.S. v. An Antique Platter of Gold*, 991 F. Supp. 222 (S.D.N.Y. 1997) aff'd, 184 F. 3d 131 (2d Cir. 1999).
48. Stephen E. Weil, "Collecting Then, Collecting Today; What's the Difference?" In *Reinventing the Museum: Historical and Contemporary Perspectives on the Paradigm Shift*, ed. Gail Anderson (Walnut Creek, CA: Alta Mira Press, 2004), 288.
49. *U.S. v. Schultz*, 333 F. 3d 393 (2nd Cir. 2003), cert. denied 2004 WL 46669 (U.S. 2004).
50. Patty Gerstenblith, "The McClain/Schultz Doctrine: Another Step against Trade in Stolen Antiquities." In *Culture Without Context* (Newsletter of the Illicit Antiquities Research Centre, Autumn 2003). 5 Dec. 2010 <http://www.mcdonald.cam.ac.uk/iarc/culturewithout-context/ issue%2013/gerstenblith.htm#545>.
51. Garner. (Definition of Scienter: 1. A degree of knowledge that makes a person legally responsible for the consequences of his or her act or omission; the fact of an act having been done knowingly. 2. A mental state consisting of an intent to deceive, manipulate, or defraud.)

52. Andrew Adler, "An Unintended and Absurd Expansion: The Application of the Archaeological Resources Protection Act to Foreign Lands," 38 *New Mexico Law Review* 133, 158 & n.151 (2008), 133–158.
53. The Archaeological Resources Protection Act. 16 U.S.C. 470ee(c) <http://www.nps.gov/history/local-law/fhpl_archrsrcsprot.pdf>.
54. The first was a successful 1997 in rem civil forfeiture claim against a vase illegally removed from Italy and was determined to violate New York theft statute: *United States v. An Archaic Etruscan Pottery Ceremonial Vase c. Late 7th Century, B.C., and a set of Rare Villanovan and Archaic Etruscan Blackware with Buchero and Impasto Ware, c. 8th–7th Century, B.C., Located at Antiquarium, Ltd., 948 Madison Avenue, New York, NY 10021*, No. 96 Civ. 9437 (S.D.N.Y. 24 Mar. 1997). The second was a 2003 case against a private collector, Taddeo Barchitta, who pled guilty to violating ARPA by dealing in antiquities defined as stolen by Peruvian law, and enforced through Virginia state theft law. *United States v. Barchitta*, No. 1:03-cr-00437 (E.D. Va. consent order of forfeiture entered 24 Sept. 2003).
55. Felch.
56. California Penal Code Section 497 makes it a violation of state law to receive property stolen in another country and to bring it into California knowing the property was stolen.
57. California Penal Code Section 31 states all persons concerned in the commission of a crime who have advised and encouraged its commission or aid and abet in its commission are principals in any crime so committed.
58. Wyatt.
59. Adler, 153.
60. Wyatt.
61. William G. Pearlstein, "Cultural Property, Congress, the Courts, and Customs: The Decline and Fall of the Antiques Market?," In *Who Owns the Past? Cultural Policy, Cultural Property, and the Law*, ed. Kate Fitz Gibbon (New Brunswick, New Jersey, and London: Rutgers University Press in association with American Council for Cultural Policy, 2005), 10.
62. Pearlstein, 10.
63. Felch, Jason, and Ralph Frammolino. "Several Museums May Possess Looted Art; Italian Prosecutors Use Photos Seized from a Convicted Trafficker of Stolen Antiquities to Identify Dozens of Suspect Objects." *Los Angeles Times*, 8 Nov. 2005, A16.
64. Michael Kimmelman, "Regarding Antiquities, Some Changes, Please," *New York Times*, 8 Dec. 2005. 12 Nov. 2010 <http://www.nytimes.com/2005/12/08/arts/08kimm.html?scp=1&sq= Regarding+Antiquities%2C+Some+Changes%2C+Please&st=nyt>.

Chapter 3

1. John Simmons in both the AAM seminar and his publication, *Things Great and Small: Collections Management Policies* (Washington, DC: American Association of Museums, 2006). Although the fundamental organization and intent behind the above steps align with the recommendations provided by John Simmons in both the AAM seminar and his publication, all the steps have been modified to meet the particularities involved with developing a policy intended to guide in the acquisition of antiquated material rather than the development of a broader collections management policy.

The AAM Registrar's Committee enabled me to attend the AAM seminar mentioned above through the Margaret A. Willard Fellowship in 2007.

2. American Association of Museums Standards Regarding Archaeological Material and Ancient Art, July 2008. 27 Nov. 2010 <http://www.aam-us.org/museumresources/ethics/upload/Standards%20Regarding%20Archaeological%20Material%20and%20Ancient%20Art.pdf> (Hereafter: AAM Standards).
3. Association of Art Museum Directors (AAMD), New Report on Acquisition of Archaeological Materials and Ancient Art, 4 June 2008. 27 Nov. 2010 <http://www.aamd.org/newsroom/documents/2008ReportAndRelease.pdf> (Hereafter: AAMD, New Report).
4. Archaeological Institute of America (AIA), Principles for Museum Acquisitions of Antiquities Mar. 2006. 12 Nov. 2007 <http://www.archaeological.org/pdfs/archaeologywatch/museumpolicy/ AIA_Principles_Musuem_Acquisition.pdf>.
5. International Council of Museums (ICOM), Ethics of Acquisitions, Apr. 1970. 12 Dec. 2007 <http://icom.museum/acquisition.html> <http://icom.museum/fileadmin/user_upload/pdf/Codes/code2006_eng.pdf> 6 July 2001. 27 Nov. 2010 (Hereafter: ICOM, Code of Ethics for Museums).
6. AAM Standards.
7. AAMD, New Report.
8. AAMD, Registry of New Acquisitions of Archaeological Material and Works of Ancient Act, 4 June 2008. 27 Nov. 2010 <http://aamdobjectregistry.org/Antiquities>.
9. AAM Standards.
10. The term "older collection" was defined by me as an example of a possible exception to basic criteria. ARPA does not use this term.
11. David Gill, "It's All the Same: The Looting of 'High Art' vs. the Looting of the Minor Arts," Looting Matters, 12 Oct. 2007. 12 Dec. 2010 <lootingmatters.blogspot.com>.
12. United Kingdom, Guidelines, 8.

Chapter 4

1. Paul Roberts, "Barriers or Bridges? Museums and Acquisitions." In *Who Owns Objects? The Ethics and Politics of Collecting Cultural Artefacts, Proceedings for the First St Cross—All Souls Seminar Series and Workshop, Oxford, October–December 2004*, eds. E. Robson, L. Treadwell, and C. Gosden (Oxford: Oxbow Books, 2006), 55–56.

Chapter 5

1. Approximately half the documentation types listed were included in the 2005 publication by the United Kingdom's Department for Culture, Media and Sport, *Combating Illicit Trade: Due Diligence Guidelines for Museums, Libraries and Archives on Collecting and Borrowing Cultural Material.*
2. These issues are covered in more detail in Marie Malaro, *A Legal Primer on Managing Museum Collections* (Washington, DC: Smithsonian, 1999).
3. The International Institute for the Unification of Private Law, UNIDROIT Convention on Stolen or Illegally Exported Cultural Objects (Rome, 1995) Article 5, Paragraph 4 <http://www.unidroit.org/english/conventions/1995culturalproperty/1995culturalpropertye.htm>.
4. United Kingdom, Guidelines.
5. Paul Roberts, "Barriers or Bridges? Museums and Acquisitions." In *Who Owns Objects? The Ethics and Politics of Collecting Cultural Artefacts, Proceedings for the First St Cross—All Souls Seminar Series and Workshop, Oxford, October–December 2004*, eds. E. Robson, L. Treadwell, and C. Gosden (Oxford: Oxbow Books, 2006), 47–59.
6. Malaro, 205–206.
7. United Kingdom, Guidelines, 9.
8. The federal investigation in California involves artificially inflated appraisals, and the affidavit cited the following federal statute: Conspiracy to Aid and Assist in the Preparation of False Tax Returns. 18 U.S.C. § 371 and 26 U.S.C. § 7206 (2).
9. Bonny MacKenzie, Affidavit to Obtain a Search Warrant for the Pacific Asia Museum, Central District of California, Docket No. 08-0118M, 22 Jan 2008. (Gabourie Langer, IRS revenue agent, cited on page 6 of report.)
10. United Kingdom Museums, Libraries & Archives Council, "Buying from On-Line Sources," Cultural Property Advice, 2006. 7 Jan. 2011 <http://www.culturalpropertyadvice.gov.uk/private_individuals/buying_with_confidence>.
11. Alan Bamberger, "Art Provenance: What Is It and How to Verify It," ArtBusiness.com, 9 Jan. 2007. 7 Jan. 2011 <http://www.artbusiness.com/

provwarn.html>. (Bamberger's recommendations concerns works of art with known artists; his recommendations have been tailored and rephrased to address archaeological and ethnographic material.)

12. United Kingdom Museums, Libraries & Archives Council, "Acceptable Evidence for Due Diligence" Cultural Property Advice, 2006. 7 Jan. 2008 <http://www.culturalpropertyadvice.gov.uk>.
13. Jessica Darraby, *Art, Artifact & Architecture Law* (Eagan, MN: Thomson/West, 2006), 78.
14. However, there are websites that provide news on international cultural property issues, such as Saving Antiquities for Everyone <http://www.savingantiquities.org> and the Museum Security Network <http://www.museum-security.org>.
15. United Kingdom, Guidelines, 10.
16. The Art Loss Register, "Benefits of Searching," 17 Nov. 2010 <https://www.artloss.com/content/searching>.
17. Trace <www.tracechecker.com>.
18. Federal Bureau of Investigation, National Stolen Art File Search, 14 Aug. 2010 < www.fbi.gov/about-us/investigate/vc_majorthefts/arttheft/arttheft>.
19. Other stolen art databases are available at <http://www.saztv.com/page9.html>.
20. Roberts, 59.
21. AAM Standards.

CHAPTER 6

1. Antiquities Act [16 U.S.C. 431-433 (1906)] <http://www.cr.nps.gov/local-law/anti1906.htm>.
2. Archaeological Resources Protection Act [16 U.S.C. §§ 470aa-470mm (1979)] (ARPA)
   ARPA statute: <http://uscode.house.gov/download/pls/16C1B.txt>
   ARPA regulation (43 CFR Part 7) <http://www.nps.gov/history/local-law/43cfr7.htm>.
3. Native American Graves Protection and Repatriation Act [Public Law 101-601, 25 U.S.C. §§ 3001-3013 (1990)]
   NAGPRA statute: http://www.access.gpo.gov/uscode/title25/chapter32_.html.
   NAGPRA website: http://www.cr.nps.gov/nagpra/.
   NAGPRA Regulations: http://www.cr.nps.gov/nagpra/MANDATES/43_CFR_10_10-1-03.pdf.
   NAGPRA Future Applicability Rule: <http://www.cr.nps.gov/nagpra/MANDATES/43_CFR_10_13_%20Final%20Rule%2003-21-07.pdf>.

4. National Park Service, Department of the Interior, Office of the Secretary, "Curation of Federally-Owned and Administered Archaeological Collections," 36 CFR 79 Federal Register 55: 37670, 12 Sep. 1990 <http://www.cr.nps.gov/archeology/tools/36cfr79.htm>.
5. Arrowheads.com, Indian Burial Laws, 2010. 4 Dec. 2010 <http://arrowheads.com/index.php/component/content/category/34>. This website summarizes the laws of all states, including thirty-eight state laws specifically addressing reburial of human skeletal remains, repatriation of human skeletal remains, and grave goods and/or unmarked grave protection statutes. The following categories of information are discussed:

> (1) who has jurisdiction for implementing the law; (2) statute of limitation in which a violator can be prosecuted; (3) types of geographical areas protected or exempted, such as mounds or designated cemeteries; (4) whether a consultation process was established; (5) if a review or consultation committee was appointed; (6) who has ultimate ownership for archaeological remains; (7) who may be held liable for prosecution for violations of the law; (8) what penalties are established; (9) whether there are exemptions to the law; and (10) if permits are required and who is responsible for issue them.

6. The National Conference of State Legislatures. State Historic Preservation Legislation Database, 1999 <http://204.131.235.67/programs/arts/statehist.htm>.
7. Indian Burial and Sacred Grounds Watch, Compilation of State Repatriation, Reburial and Grave Protection Laws, 10 Feb. 2011 <http://www.ibsgwatch.imagedjinn.com/learn/lawsstate.htm>.
8. Carol L. Carnett, *A Survey of State Statutes Protecting Archeological Resources*. (The third in the Archeological Assistance Study series, it was published in August 1995 by the National Trust for Historic Preservation and the U.S. Department of the Interior National Park Service, Cultural Resources, Archeological Assistance Division.)
9. The National Conference of State Historic Preservation Officers <http://www.ncshpo.org/find/index.htm>.
10. Julia Miller, *A Layperson's Guide to Historic Preservation Law* (Washington, DC: National Trust for Historic Preservation, 1997), 16.
11. U.S. Department of the Interior. National Park Service. Native American Graves Protection and Repatriation Act. NAGPRA Glossary, 14 Feb. 2011 <http://www.cr.nps.gov/nagpra/TRAINING/GLOSSARY.HTM >.
12. NAGPRA. Sec. 1170 Illegal Trafficking in Native American Human Remains and Cultural Items <http://www.cr.nps.gov/local-law/FHPL_NAGPRA.pdf>.
13. NAGPRA, Glossary.

14. Gary Edson and David Dean, *The Handbook for Museums* (New York and London: Routledge, 1996), 30.
15. The $5,000 value is determined by NSPA, which makes it a crime to knowingly possess a stolen item worth more than $5,000 and transport it across state lines. This law has been used to prosecute cases of dealing in cultural property in instances where the dealer knew the object was stolen. It is covered in more detail in Chapter 2.
16. National Atlas of the United States of America <http://nationalatlas.gov/printable/fedlands.html#mo>.
17. Websites providing news on international cultural property issues, such as Saving Antiquities for Everyone <http://www.savingantiquities.org> and the Museum Security Network <http://www.museum-security.org> may cover such activity.
18. Indian Burials and Sacred Grounds Watch <http://www.ibsgwatch.imagedjinn.com/learn/ learn2.htm#parks>. This information was collected from the National Register of Historic Places Database through a search for "mound." NRHP database <http://www.nps.gov/nr/research/>.
19. The National Conference of State Historic Preservation Officers website is available at: <http://www.ncshpo.org/find/index.htm>.
20. The National Association of Tribal Historic Preservation Officers website is available at: <http://www.nathpo.org/THPO_Members/state_list.htm>.
21. The National Association of State Archaeologists website is available at: <http://www.nathpo.org/map.html>.

Chapter 7

1. Pre-Columbian Monumental, Architectural Sculpture or Murals Act [19 U.S.C §§2091-2095] Regulations: [19 CFR §§12.105-12.109 (1972)] <http://exchanges.state.gov/culprop/92-587.html>.
2. United States Customs, 15.
3. Convention on Cultural Property Implementation Act [19 U.S.C §§ 2601-2613], CPIA Regulations: [19 CFR §§ 12.104-12.104i. (1982)].
4. Current and expired CPIA agreements: <http://exchanges.state.gov/culprop/list.html>.
5. CPIA-restricted material image database: <http://exchanges.state.gov/culprop/database.html>.
6. United States Customs, 19.
7. The following is the list of treaties and executive agreements mentioned by Jessica Darraby on page 351 of *Art, Artifact & Architecture Law*:

   1. Treaty of Cooperation between the United States of America and the United Mexican States Providing for the Recovery and Return of Stolen

Archaeological, Historical, and Cultural Properties, 17 July 1970 (22 U.S.T. 494). 2. Agreement between the United States and Republic of Peru for Recovery and Return of Stolen Archaeological, Historical and Cultural Properties. Entered into force 15 Sept. 1981 (T.I.A.S. No. 10136, 33 U.S.T. 1608). 3. Agreement between the United States and the Republic of Guatemala for Recovery and Return of Stolen Archaeological, Historical and Cultural Properties, 21 May 1984, entered into force 12 Aug. 1984 (T.I.A.S. No. 11077). 4. Agreement between the United States and Ecuador for Recovery and Return of Stolen Archaeological, Historical and Cultural Properties. 12, Nov. 1983, entered into force 14 Jan. 1987 (T.I.A.S. No. 11075).

8. Treaty of Cooperation between the United States of America and the United Mexican States Providing for the Recovery and Return of Stolen Archaeological, Historical, and Cultural Properties, 17 July 1970 (22 U.S.T. 494, Article 1).
9. United States Department of the Treasury, Sanctions Program, 21 Feb. 2011 <http://www.treasury.gov/resource-center/sanctions/Programs/Pages/Programs.aspx>.
10. International Foundation for Art Research (IFAR), International Cultural Property/Ownership & Export Legislation (ICPOEL), 19 Nov. 2010 <http://www.ifar.org/icpoel.php>. Considered the most comprehensive and up-to-date resource.
11. The UNESCO Cultural Heritage Laws Database provides links to many foreign cultural property laws. A number of the cultural property laws are provided only in the country of origin's language. The effective date of the legislation is not always discernable. This site is updated as UNESCO is informed of applicable laws and should be consulted prior to acquiring foreign cultural material <http://www.unesco.org/culture/natlaws/index.php?&lng=en>.
12. The UNESCO Publication, *Handbook of National Regulations Concerning the Export of Cultural Property*, prepared by Lyndel Prott and Patrick O'Keefe in 1988, provides useful summaries of legislation in force on 31 Dec. 1987 <http://unesdoc.unesco.org/images/0011/001191/119126eo.pdf>.
13. *The Collection of Legislative Texts Concerning the Protection of Movable Cultural Property* is a compilation of separate booklets listing legislation for twenty-five countries. These booklets were published by UNESCO from 1985 to 1988. Each booklet contains a summary page that serves as an index to the following legislation. The booklets can be accessed by searching the UNESCO website <http://unesdoc.unesco.org/ulis/index.shtml> for: "Collection of Legislative Texts Concerning the Protection of Movable Cultural Property" followed by the country in question.
14. A list of state parties to the1970 UNESCO Convention on the Means of Prohibiting and Preventing the Illicit Import, Export and Transfer

of Ownership of Cultural Property, 19 Nov. 2010 <http://portal.unesco.org/la/convention.asp?KO=13039&language=E&order=alpha>. (This list is subject to change.)

15. United States Customs, 14.
16. United States Customs, 14.
17. United States Customs, 14.
18. United States Customs, 19.
19. Department of Homeland Security, U.S. Customs and Border Protection, Entry Summary (CBP Form 7501), June 2009, 19 Nov. 2010 <http://forms.cbp.gov/pdf/CBP_Form_7501.pdf>.
20. Merriam-Webster defines a pro forma invoice as "a document provided prior to or with a shipment of goods (as for export) that describes the items and terms of sale but does not have the function of a real invoice," 19 Nov. 2010 <http://www.merriam-webster.com/dictionary/pro+forma+invoice>.
21. These instructions are loosely based on questions provided in "The Metropolitan Museum of Art", "Customs Paperwork Required for Acquisitions," and "Worksheet for Acquisitions of Art and Antiquities" provided by Rebecca L. Murray, associate council for the MET, in course materials for "Acquisition Best Practices," *ALI-ABA Course of Study, Legal Issues in Museum Administration* (Philadelphia: American Law Institute, American Bar Association, 14–16 Mar. 2007). However, the information has been updated to reflect the revised organization of the CBP Form 7501, which was updated in June 2009.
22. United Kingdom, Guidelines, 8.
23. Association of Art Museum Directors, "Art Museums and the International Exchange of Cultural Artifacts," Oct. 2001. 28 Nov. 2010 <http://www.aamd.org/papers/documents/CulturalProperty_000.pdf>.
24. The UNESCO World Heritage in Danger List <http://whc.unesco.org/en/danger/>. The countries containing these endangered sites are coded as "D" in Table E.2 in Appendix E.
25. The ICOM website provides information on the listed endangered cultural resources, <http://icom.museum/redlist/index.html>.The countries of origin for items included on the ICOM Red List are coded as "R" in Table E.2 in Appendix E.
26. <http://www.ifar.org/icpoel.php>.
27. See note 11, this chapter.
28. Foreign Consular Offices in the United States can be searched through the U.S. Department of State <http://www.state.gov/s/cpr/rls/fco/69458.htm>.
29. UNESCO field offices <http://portal.unesco.org/en/ev.php-URL_ID=34016&URL_DO=DO_TOPIC&URL_ SECTION=201.html>.

CHAPTER 8

1. Stephen E. Weil, "From Being *about* Something to Being *for* Somebody: The Ongoing Transformation of the American Museum," *Daedalus* 128:3 (Summer 1999), 239.
2. Rubie Watson, "Culturally Sensitive Collections: A Museum Perspective." In *Stewards of the Sacred*, eds. Lawrence E. Sullivan and Alison Edwards (Washington, DC and Cambridge, MA: American Association of Museums and Harvard University Center for the Study of World Religions, 2004), 120.
3. Ken Gewertz, "A Totem Pole Comes Home: Tlingit Artifact Is Returned to Alaska," *Harvard Gazette*, 19 July 2001.
4. Barbara Kirshenblatt-Gimblett, "Objects of Ethnography." In *The Ethics of Collecting Cultural Property: Whose Culture? Whose Property?*, ed. Phyllis Mauch Messenger (Albuquerque, University of New Mexico Press, 1990), 391.
5. Kirshenblatt-Gimblett, 391.
6. James Cuno, "Why Art Museums Are Essential." In *Stewards of the Sacred*, eds. Alison Edwards and Lawrence E. Sullivan (Washington, DC and Cambridge, MA: American Association of Museums and Harvard University Center for the Study of World Religions, 2004), 34.
7. AAM, Code of Ethics.
8. Association of Art Museum Directors, Report on the Stewardship and Acquisition of Sacred Objects, 9 Aug. 2006. 12 Dec. 2010 <http://www.aamd.org/papers/documents/SacredObjectsReleaseand GuidelinesCombined8.9.06dated.pdf>.
9. Mark O'Neill, "Enlightenment Museums: Universal or Merely Global?," *Museum and Society* 2(3), Nov. 2004, 193. <http://www.le.ac.uk/ms/m&s/Issue%206/ONeill.pdf>.
10. O'Neill, 193.
11. "Declaration on the Importance and Value of Universal Museums," Cleveland Museum of Art, Dec. 2002. 20 Feb. 2008 http://www.clevelandart.org/museum/info/CMA206_Mar7_03.pdf:

    The international museum community shares the conviction that illegal traffic in archaeological, artistic, and ethnic objects must be firmly discouraged. We should, however, recognize that objects acquired in earlier times must be viewed in the light of different sensitivities and values, reflective of that earlier era.

    (Note: in his article, O'Neill (2004, 190–202) commented that the "initial reaction to the Declaration was summarized by The Art Newspaper under the headline: 'A George Bush approach to international relations" [Bailey, 2003, 7]).

12. Holland Cotter, "Who Owns Art?," *New York Times*, 29 Mar. 2006. 14 Feb. 2011 <www.elginism.com/20060330/372/print>.
13. George E. Hein, *Learning in the Museum* (London and New York: Routledge, 1998), 177. (Author referenced J. Luska, "Inside the Inside Story," *Museum News*, 75[2]: 24–25, 72–73.)
14. Lesley Bone, "Teotihuacan Mural Project," *WAAC Newsletter* 8:3 (Sept. 1986), 2–7. 22 Feb. 2011 <http://palimpsest.stanford.edu/waac/wn/wn08/wn08-3/wn08-301.html>.
15. Kathleen Berrin, "Fine Arts Museums of San Francisco Acquire Maya Stela," *P.A.R.I. Online Publications Newsletter* 28 (June 1999), 22 Feb. 2011. <http://www.mesoweb.com/pari/publications/news_archive/28/fine_arts_stela.html>.
16. Berrin.
17. The Menil Collection, The Byzantine Fresco Chapel Museum, 18 Feb. 2008 <http://www.menil.org/collection/byzantine.php>.
18. Mark Rose, "Special Report: Church Treasures of Cyprus," *Archaeology* 51:4 (July/Aug. 1998), 4.
19. Colin Renfrew, *Loot, Legitimacy and Ownership: The Ethical Crisis in Archaeology* (Amsterdam: Joh. Enschede, 1999), 12.
20. Museo Tumbas Reales de Sipán, 12 Feb. 2011 < http://www.tumbas-reales.org/>.

TABLE 1.1

1. Theresa L. Leming, "Dead Bodies," *American Jurisprudence* 2nd ed., 2008. 22A §3.
2. Marie Malaro, *A Legal Primer on Managing Museum Collections* (Washington, DC: Smithsonian, 1999).

TABLE 6.6

1. United Kingdom Guidelines (October 2005) <http://www.culture.gov.uk/Reference_ library/Publications/archive_2005/illicit_trade.htm>.

TABLE 7.2

1. United States Customs, 15.

TABLE 7.3

1. United States Customs, 15.

Table 7.7

1. United Kingdom, Guidelines.

Table 7.8

1. Jessica Darraby, *Art, Artifact and Archaeology Law* (Eagan, MN: Thomson/West, 2006, 361), may be helpful for museums seeking to determine the likelihood of a foreign cultural property law being upheld in U.S. courts.

Table C.1

1. United Kingdom, Guidelines.

Table D.1

1. United States Customs, 15.
2. United States Customs, 15.
3. United Kingdom, Guidelines.

Table E.1

1. Country names sometimes reflect a national identity in existence at the time agreements, treaties, etc., are created, but which are no longer known by the same name (i.e., the Soviet Union); the status of laws within those countries is beyond the scope of this book. Museums should seek legal counsel for items originating from countries that no longer exist.
2. Convention on Cultural Property Implementation Act [19 U.S.C §§ 2601-2613, Regulations: 19 CFR §§ 12.104-12.104i. (1982)].
3. Pre-Columbian Monumental, Architectural Sculpture or Murals Act [19 U.S.C §§2091-2095] Regulations: 19 CFR §§12.105-12.109 (1972) <http://exchanges.state.gov/culprop/92-587.html>.
4. United States Customs, 14, 20–22.
5. Treaty of Cooperation between the United States of America and the United Mexican States Providing for the Recovery and Return of Stolen Archaeological, Historical, and Cultural Properties, 17 July 1970, 22 U.S.T. 494.
6. Agreement between the United States and Republic of Peru for Recovery and Return of Stolen Archaeological, Historical, and Cultural Properties, 15 Sept. 1981 (T.I.A.S. No. 10136, 33 U.S.T. 1608).

7. Agreement between the United States and the Republic of Guatemala for Recovery and Return of Stolen Archaeological, Historical, and Cultural Properties, 21 May 1984, entered into force 12 Aug. 1984 (T.I.A.S. No. 11077).
8. Agreement between the United States and Ecuador for Recovery and Return of Stolen Archaeological, Historical, and Cultural Properties, entered into force 14 Jan. 1987 (T.I.A.S. No. 11075).
9. International Foundation for Art Research. International Cultural Property/Ownership & Export Legislation (ICPOEL).< http://www.ifar.org/icpoel.php> (last viewed 20 Nov. 2011). [Now considered the most accessible and comprehensive listing of applicable. Subject to update.]
10. See note 11, Chapter 7.
11. The UNESCO publication, *Handbook of National Regulations Concerning the Export of Cultural Property*, prepared by Lyndel Prott and Patrick O'Keefe in 1988, provides useful summaries of legislation in force on 31 Dec. 1987.
12. See note 13, Chapter 7.
13. A complete list of state parties to the 1970 UNESCO Convention on the Means of Prohibiting and Preventing the Illicit Import, Export, and Transfer of Ownership of Cultural Property can be found at <http://portal.unesco.org/la/convention.asp?KO=13039&language=E>. This website should be reviewed for updates regularly if ratification or acceptance of the convention is a determining factor in the museum's review process. Table E.2 updated as of 20 Feb. 2011.
14. The ICOM Red List includes "cultural goods most affected by looting and theft" from Africa, Latin America, Iraq, and Afghanistan, Peru, Mexico, and Central America. More information on the cultural resources listed can be found at <http://icom.museum/redlist/index.html> and <http://icom.museum/what-we-do/programmes/fighting-illicit-traffic/red-list.html>.
15. The UNESCO World Heritage in Danger List includes thirty sites that the World Heritage Committee has included on the List of World Heritage in danger in accordance with Article 11 (4) of the 1972 World Heritage Convention. The World Heritage Committee can inscribe on the List of World Heritage in Danger properties whose protection requires "major operations" and for which assistance has been requested. This list can be found at <http://whc.unesco.org/en/danger/> (15 Feb. 2011).

Bibliography

Adler, Andrew. "An Unintended and Absurd Expansion: The Application of the Archaeological Resources Protection Act to Foreign Lands." *New Mexico Law Review* 38 (2008): 133, 158 & n.151.

Adler, Andrew L., and Stephen W. Clark. "Update: Repatriation/Antiquities Disputes of 2006." *ALI-ABA Course of Study, Legal Issues in Museum Administration.* Philadelphia: American Law Institute and American Bar Association, 14–16 Mar. 2007.

American Association of Museums. "American Association of Museums Code of Ethics," 2000. 12 Feb. 2011<http://www.aam-us.org/museumresources/ethics/coe.cfm>.

———. "Americans Identify a Source of Information They Can Really Trust," 7 May 2001. American Association of Museums website, 7 Aug. 2010<http://www.aam-us.org/pressreleases.cfm?mode=list&id=21>.

———. Excellence and Equity: Education and the Public Dimension of Museums. Washington, DC: American Association of Museums, 1992.

———. Registrars Committee website. 27 Nov. 2010<http://www.rcaam.org>.

———. Standards Regarding Archaeological Material and Ancient Art, July 2008. 27 Nov. 2010<http://www.aam-us.org/museumresources/ethics/upload/ Standards%20 Regarding%20Archaeological%20Material%20and%20Ancient%20Art.pdf>.

American Institute of Archaeology. "American Institute of Archaeology Code of Ethics," 29 Dec. 1997. American Institute of Archaeology website, 7 June 2010<http://www.archaeological.org/news/advocacy/130>.

"Ancient Wreath Returns to Greece," 30 Mar. 2007. *BBC News*, 22 Dec. 2007<http://news.bbc.co.uk/2/hi/europe/6505971.stm>.

Archaeological Resources Protection Act, The. Pub. L. 96-95. 16 U.S.C. 470aa-mm, 31 Oct. 1979. 10 Feb. 2011<http://www.nps.gov/history/local-law/fhpl_archrsrcsprot.pdf>.

Arrowheads.com, Indian Burial Laws, 2010. 4 Dec. 2010<http://arrowheads.com/index.php/component/content/category/34>.

Arroyo, Leah. "Getty Battles Could Set Precedent." *AVISO* 31 (Dec. 2005): 1. [American Association of Museums newsletter].

Art Loss Registry. 16 Feb. 2011<http://www.artloss.com>.

Association of Art Museum Directors. "Art Museums and the International Exchange of Cultural Artifacts," Oct. 2001. 7 Aug. 2007<http://www.aamd.org/papers>.

———. New Report on Acquisition of Archaeological Materials and Ancient Art, 4 June 2008. 27 Nov. 2010<http://www.aamd.org/newsroom/documents/2008 ReportAndRelease.pdf>.

Association of Art Museum Directors. Registry of New Acquisitions of Archaeological Material and Works of Ancient Art, 4 June 2008. 27 Nov. 2010<http://aamdobjectregistry.org/Antiquities>.

———. "Report of the AAMD Task Force on the Acquisition and Stewardship of Sacred Objects." 1 June 2006. 7 Aug. 2010<http://www.aamd.org/papers/>.

———. "Report of the AAMD Task Force on the Acquisition of Archaeological Materials and Ancient Art." 4 June 2004. 7 Aug. 2007<http://www.aamd.org/papers/>.

Bamberger, Alan. "Art Provenance: What Is It and How to Verify It." 2005. ArtBusiness.com. 9 Jan. 2010<http://www.artbusiness.com/provwarn.html>.

Bator, Paul M. *The International Trade in Art*. Chicago: University of Chicago Press, Midway Reprint, 1988.

Bator, Paul M., and John Merryman. "The Nation and the Object." *International Journal of Cultural Property* 3 (1994): 61–76.

Berrin, Kathleen. "Fine Arts Museums of San Francisco Acquire Maya Stele: Collaboration with Guatemala and Mexico Sets New Standards for Museums." *P.A.R.I. Online Publications Newsletter* 28 (June 1999)<http://www.mesoweb.com/pari/publications/news_archive/28/fine_arts_stela.html>.

Bibas, Steven A. "The Case against Statutes of Limitation for Stolen Art." *Yale Law Journal* 103 (1993–1994): 2442.

Bone, Lesley. "Teotihuacán Mural Project." *WAAC Newsletter* 8:3 (Sept. 1986): 2–7. 12 Feb. 2011<http://palimpsest.stanford.edu/waac/wn/wn08/wn08-3/wn08-301.html>.

Brodie, Neil, J. Doole, and P. Watson. *Stealing History: The Illicit Trade in Cultural Material*. Cambridge, UK: McDonald Institute for Archaeological Research, 2000.

Brodie, Neil, and Colin Renfrew. "Looting and the World's Archaeological Heritage: The Inadequate Response." *Annual Review of Anthropology* 34 (Oct. 2005): 343–361.

Brodie, Neil, and Kathryn Walker Tubb. *Illicit Antiquities: The Theft of Culture and the Extinction of Archaeology*. London, New York: Routledge, 2002.

Brown, Michael F. *Who Owns Native Culture?* Cambridge, MA: Harvard University Press, 2003.

Buck, Rebecca, and Jean Gilmore. *The New Museum Registration Methods*. Washington, DC: American Association of Museums, 1998.

Burke, Barlow. *Personal Property in a Nutshell*. 3rd ed. St. Paul, MN: Thomson West, 2003.

Burr, Sherri, Leonard D. DuBoff, and Michael Murray. *Art Law: Cases and Materials*. Buffalo, NY: William S. Hein Publishing, 2004.

Butler, William B. *State Archaeological Education Programs*. Denver: National Park Service, Rocky Mountain Region, Division of National Preservation Programs, Interagency Archeological Services, 1992.

Carassava, Anthee. "Greek Count Dismisses Case against Ex Curator." nytimes.com, 28 Nov. 2007<http://www.nytimes.com/2007/ 11/28/arts/design/28true.html?ex=1353906000&en=1e696d4155674ad8&ei=5124&partner=permalink&exprod=permalink>.

Carducci, Guido. "The Growing Complexity of International Art Law." In *Art and Cultural Heritage: Law, Policies and Practices*, edited by B. Hoffman, 68–85. Cambridge, UK: Cambridge University Press, 2005.

Carnett, Carol L. *A Survey of State Statutes Protecting Archaeological Resources*. Archaeological Assistance Study Number 3. U.S. Department of the Interior, National Park Service, Cultural Resources Program and the National Trust for Historic Preservation, Aug. 1995.

Clapp, James E. *Webster's Legal Dictionary*. New York: Random House, 1996.

Coggins, Clemency. "Archaeology and the Art Market." *Science* 175 (1972): 263–268.

———. "Illicit Traffic in Pre-Columbian Antiquities." *Art Journal* 29 (1969): 94.

College Art Association. "Resolution Concerning the Acquisition of Cultural Properties Originating in Foreign Countries," April 1973. 12 Dec. 2010<http://www.collegeart.org/guidelines/cultpropres.html>.

Convention on Cultural Property Implementation Act. [19 USC §§ 2601-2613], CPIA Regulations: [19 CFR §§ 12.104-12.104i. (1982)].

Cotter, Holland. "Who Owns Art?" *New York Times*, 29 Mar. 2006. 14 Feb. 2010<www.elginism.com/20060330/372/print>.

Cunningham, Richard B. *Archaeology, Relics and the Law*. 2nd ed. Durham, NC: Carolina Academic Press, 2005.

Cuno, James B. "Why Art Museums Are Essential." In *Stewards of the Sacred*, edited by Alison Edwards and Lawrence E. Sullivan, 33–40. Washington, DC: American Association of Museums in cooperation with the Center for the Study of World Religions, Harvard University, 2004.

Darraby, Jessica L. *Art, Artifact & Architecture Law*. Eagan, MN: Thomson/West, 2006.

Dean, David, and Gary Edson. *The Handbook for Museums*. New York and London: Routledge, 1996.

DeAngelis, Ildiko P. "How Much Provenance Is Enough? Post-Schultz Guidelines for Art Museum Acquisition of Archaeological Materials and Ancient Art." In *Art and Cultural Heritage: Law, Policies and Practices*, edited by Barbara Hoffman, 398–408. Cambridge, UK: Cambridge University Press, 2005.

"Declaration on the Importance and Value of Universal Museums," Dec. 2002. 20 Feb. 2011<http://www.tomflynn.co.uk/UniversalMuseumsDeclaration.pdf>.

Duerksen, Christopher J., ed. *A Handbook on Historic Preservation Law*. Washington, DC: The Conservation Foundation and the National Center for Preservation Law, 1983.

Eakin, Hugh. "Italy Focuses on a Princeton Curator in an Antiquities Investigation." nytimes.com, 2 June 2010<http://www.nytimes.com/2010/06/03/arts/design/03curator.html>.

Eakin, Hugh, and Randy Kennedy. "The Met, Ending 30-Year Stance, Is Set to Yield Prized Vase to Italy." nytimes.com, 3 Feb. 2006. 24 Dec. 2010<http://www.nytimes.com/2006/02/02/arts/02cnd-museum.html>.

Edwards, Alison, and Lawrence Sullivan, eds. *Stewards of the Sacred*. Washington, DC: American Association of Museums in cooperation with the Center for the Study of World Religions, Harvard University, 2004.

Ehrehard, John E., and George S. Smith, eds. *Protecting the Past*. Southeast Archeological Center, 3 Aug. 2000. 12 Feb. 2011<http://www.cr.nps.gov/seac/protecting/>.

Elia, Ricardo J. "A Move in the Right Direction." *Art Newspaper Archives* Record Number 17470 (July 2011)<http://62.253.251.9/access/artnewspaper.html>.

Elsen, Albert E., John Henry Merryman, and Stephen K. Urice. *Law, Ethics and the Visual Arts*. 5th ed. The Netherlands: Klewer Law International B.V., 2007.

Fagan, Brian. *Archaeology*. 6th ed. New York: Longman, 1997.

Federal Bureau of Investigation. Art Theft Program, 14 Aug. 2007<http://www.fbi.gov/hq/cid/arttheft/noticerecov.htm>.

Felch, Jason. "Raids Suggest a Deeper Network of Looted Art." *Los Angeles Times*, 25 Jan. 2008. 3 Feb. 2008<http://www.latimes.com/news/loca/la-me-museums25jan25,0,101198.story>.

Felch, Jason, and Mike Boehm. "Chicagoan's Collection Target in Looted Art Probe." chicagotribune.com, 30 Jan. 2008. 13 Feb. 2008<http://www.chicagotribune.com/news/chi-museum_30jan30, 0,7058466,print.story>.

Felch, Jason, and Ralph Frammolino. "Several Museums May Possess Looted Art; Italian Prosecutors Use Photos Seized from a Convicted Trafficker of Stolen Antiquities to Identify Dozens of Suspect Objects." *Los Angeles Times*, 8 Nov. 2005, A16.

Fowler, John M. "The Legal Structure for the Protection of Archaeological Resources." In *Protecting the Past*, edited by G. Smith and J. Ehrehard. Atlanta: National Park Service, Southeast Archeological Center, 3 Aug. 2000. 7 Aug. 2010<http://www.cr.nps.gov/seac/protecting/word/2a-fowler.doc>.

Fox News. "Fed Agents Raid California Museums for Looted Artifacts," 24 Jan. 2008. 3 Feb. 2010<http://www.foxnews.com/story/0,2933,325405,00.html#ixzz17G6v77p4>.

Garner, Bryan, ed. *Black's Law Dictionary*. 8th ed. St. Paul, MN: West Group, 2004.

Gerstenblith, Patty. "An Internationally Respectful Application of National Law." *The Art Newspaper* Jan. 2004: 143.

———. *Art, Cultural Heritage, and the Law: Cases and Materials*. Durham, NC: Carolina Academic Press, 2004.

Gewertz, Ken. "A Totem Pole Comes Home: Tlingit Artifact Is Returned to Alaska." *Harvard Gazette* (19 July 2001)<http://news.harvard.edu/gazette/legacy-gazette/#>.

Gill, David. "Due Diligence Procedures Not Enough to Satisfy Them." Looting Matters, 17 Aug. 2007. 18 Sept. 2007<http://lootingmatters.blogspot.com>.

———. "Illicit Antiquities: What Are the Issues?" Looting Matters, 3 Aug. 2007. 19 Sept. 2007<http://lootingmatters.blogspot.com/2007/08/illicit-antiquities-what-are-issues.html>.

———. "It's All the Same: The Looting of 'High Art' vs. the Looting of the Minor Arts." Looting Matters, 12 Oct. 2007 <lootingmatters.blogspot.com>.

Govt. of Peru v. Johnson, 720 F. Supp. 810 (S.D. Cal 1989) aff'd, 933 F. 2d 1013 (9th Cir. 1991).

Hein, George E. *Learning in the Museum*. London and New York: Routledge, 1998.

Henry, S. *Protecting Archaeological Sites on Private Lands*. Washington, DC: National Park Service, 1993.

Hoffman, Barbara, ed. *Art and Cultural Heritage: Law, Policies and Practices*. Cambridge, UK: Cambridge University Press, 2005.

Hutt, Sherry. *Cultural Property Law: A Practitioner's Guide to the Management, Protection, and Preservation*. Chicago: Section of Environment, Energy, and Resources, American Bar Association, 2004.

Hutt, Sherry, et al. *Archeological Resource Protection*. Washington, DC: National Trust for Historic Preservation, Preservation Press, 1992.

Indian Burial and Sacred Grounds Watch Website. 2000–2003. 7 Aug. 2010<http://www.ibsgwatch.imagedjinn.com/learn/lawsstate.htm>.

International Council of Museums. ICOM Code of Ethics. Oct. 2004. 7 Aug. 2010<http://icom.museum/who-we-are/the-vision/code-of-ethics.html>.

———. ICOM Red List, The. 14 Feb. 2011<http://icom.museum/redlist/index.html> and <http://archives.icom.museum/redlist/index.html>.

International Foundation for Art Research. 7 Dec. 2010<http://www.ifar.org>.

———. Collector's Corner. 7 Dec. 2010<http://www.ifar.org/collectors_corner.php>.

———. International Cultural Property/Ownership & Export Legislation (ICPOEL). 7 Dec. 2010<http://www.ifar.org/icpoel.php>.

International Institute for the Unification of Private Law. The UNIDROIT Convention on Stolen or Illegally Exported Cultural Objects sponsored by the International Institute for the Unification of Private Law. 1995. 14 Feb. 2011<www.unidroit.org/english/conventions/1995culturalproperty/main.htm>.

J. Paul Getty Museum. "The J. Paul Getty Museum Announces Revised Acquisitions Policy." J. Paul Getty Museum Press Releases. 26 Oct. 2006. 17 Dec. 2010<http://www.getty.edu/news/press/center/revised_acquisition_policy_release_102 606.html>.

J. Paul Getty Trust. "J. Paul Getty Museum Acquisition Policy." J. Paul Getty Trust Governance website. 26 Oct. 2006. 17 Dec. 2010<http://www.getty.edu/about/governance/policies.html>.

Kennedy, Randy. "Getty Agrees to Return 40 Antiquities to Italy." *New York Times*, 2 Aug. 2007, Late edition, final, E1.

———. "Yale and Peruvian Officials Agree on Return of Artifacts." *New York Times*, 17 Sept. 2007, E3.

Kimmelman, Michael. "Critic's Notebook: Regarding Antiquities, Some Changes, Please." *New York Times*, 8 Dec. 2005<http://query.nytimes.com/gst/fullpage.html?res=9B0CE0DD1031F93BA35751C1A9639C8B63&pagewanted=all>.

Kirshenblatt-Gimblett, Barbara. "Objects of Ethnography." In *Exhibiting Cultures: The Poetics and Politics of Museum Display*, edited by Ivan Karp and Steven D. Lavine, 386–443. Washington, DC and London: Smithsonian Institution Press, 1990.

Law.com Law Dictionary. 14 Feb. 2011<http://dictionary.law.com/>.

Leming, Theresa L. "Dead Bodies." *American Jurisprudence*. 2nd ed. 22A §3, 2008.

Litt, Stephen. "Cleveland Museum of Art Will Return Tainted Antiquities to Italy Wednesday." 21 Apr. 2009. 3 Dec. 2010<http://www.cleveland.com/arts/index.ssf/2009/04/cleveland_museum_of_art_will_r.html>.

MacKenzie, Bonny. Affidavit to Obtain a Search Warrant for the Pacific Asia Museum, Central District of California, Docket No. 08-0118M. 22 Jan. 2008.

Mackenzie, Simon R. M. *Going, Going, Gone: Regulating the Market in Illicit Antiquities*. Leicester, UK: Institute of Art and Law, 2005, 6.

Malaro, Marie. *A Legal Primer on Managing Museum Collections*. Washington, DC: Smithsonian, 1999.

Martindale-Hubbell Law Digest: U.S. States, U.S. Federal, U.S. Copyright, Patent, Trademark. New Providence, NJ: LexisNexis, 2006.

McAllister, Martin E. "Looting and Vandalism of Archaeological Resources on Federal and Indian Lands in the United States." In *Protecting the Past*, edited by G. Smith and J. Ehrehard. Atlanta: National Park Service, Southeast Archeological Center, 3 Aug. 2000. 7 Aug. 2007<http://www.cr.nps.gov/seac/protecting/html/3c-mcallister.htm>.

McManamon, Francis P., and Susan D. Morton. "Reducing the Illegal Trafficking in Antiquities." In *Cultural Resource Management in Contemporary Society: Perspectives on Managing and Presenting the Past*, edited by Alf Hatton and Francis P. McManamon, 247–275. Routledge, London and New York, 2003.

Menil Collection, The. The Byzantine Fresco Chapel Museum. 18 Feb. 2011<http://www.menil.org/byzantine.html>.

Merryman, John Henry. *Law, Ethics, and the Visual Arts*. 5th edition. Alphen aan den Rijn, The Netherlands, and Frederick, MD: Kluwer Law International, 2007.

Metropolitan Museum of Art, The. "Customs Paperwork Required for Acquisitions" and "Worksheet for Acquisitions of Art and Antiquities," provided by Rebecca L. Murray, associate council for the MET, in course materials for "Acquisition Best Practices," ALI-ABA Course of Study, Legal Issues in Museum Administration. Philadelphia, American Law Institute, and the American Bar Association, 14–16 Mar. 2007.

———. "Sample Warranty and Indemnification," provided by Rebecca L. Murray, associate council for the MET, in course materials for "Acquisition Best Practices," ALI-ABA Course of Study, Legal Issues in Museum Administration. Philadelphia, American Law Institute, and the American Bar Association, 14–16 Mar. 2007.

Meyer, Karl E. *The Plundered Past*. New York: Atheneum, 1973.

Miller, Julia H. *A Layperson's Guide to Historic Preservation Law: A Survey of Federal, State, and Local Laws Governing Historic Resource Protection*. Washington, DC: National Trust for Historic Preservation, 1997.

Museo Tumbas Reales de Sipán. 12 Feb. 2011<http://www.tumbasreales.org/>.

Museum of Fine Arts, Boston. "Deputy Prime Minister of Italy Unveils Ancient Masterpiece on Loan to the Museum of Fine Arts, Boston." 28 Nov. 2006. Museum of Fine Arts, Boston, Press Releases, 16 Jan. 2008<http://www.mfa.org/about/sub.asp?key=82&subkey=3797>.

Museum Security Network. 14 Feb. 2011< http://www.museum-security.org>.

National Association of State Archaeologists, The. 19 Dec. 2010<http://www.uiowa.edu/~osa/nasa/>.

National Association of Tribal Historic Preservation Officers, The. 19 Dec. 2010<www.nathpo.org>.

National Atlas of the United States of America. 19 Dec. 2010<http://nationalatlas.gov/printable/fedlands.html#mo>.

National Conference of State Historic Preservation Officers, The. 19 Dec. 2010<www.ncshpo.org/>.

National Conference of State Legislatures. State Historic Preservation Legislation Database. 1999. 20 Feb. 2011<http://204.131.235.67/programs/arts/statehist.htm>.

O'Keefe, Patrick J. "Museum Acquisition Policies and the UNESCO Convention." *Museum International* 50 (Jan. 1998): 20–21.

O'Neill, Mark. "Enlightenment Museums: Universal or Merely Global?" *Museum and Society* 2 (4 Sept. 2007): 3.<http://www.le.ac.uk/ms/m&s/Issue%206/ ONeill.pdf>.

Parker, Lori J. "Proof of a Claim Involving Stolen Art or Antiquities." *American Jurisprudence Proof of Facts*. 3rd ed. 77 (2005): 259.

Pearlstein, William G. "Cultural Property, Congress, the Courts, and Customs: The Decline and Fall of the Antiquities Market?" In *Who Owns the Past? Cultural Policy, Cultural Property, and the Law*, edited by Kate Fitz Gibbon, 9–27. New Brunswick, NJ and London: Rutgers University Press in association with American Council for Cultural Policy, 2005.

Phelan, Marilyn. "Legal and Ethical Considerations in Museum Acquisitions." In *Museum Philosophy for the Twenty-First Century*, edited by H. H. Genoways, 27–46. Oxford, UK: AltaMira Press, 2006.

Phoebe A. Hearst Museum of Anthropology. Donation of Artifacts Questionnaire. Apr. 2005. 14 Feb. 2011<http://hearstmuseum.berkeley.edu/collections/pdfs/donation_form.pdf>.

Povoledo, Elisabetta. "An Impasse in Italian Talks over Return of Artifacts." nytimes.com, 26 May 2007.

———. "Boston Museum Returns 13 Ancient Works to Italy." nytimes.com, 29 Sept. 2006.

———. "Collector Returns Art Italy Says Was Looted." nytimes.com, 18 Jan. 2008.

———."Confrontation Looms at the Met." *New York Times*, 21 Nov. 2005, E1.

———. "Italy Makes Its Choices of Antiquities to Lend MET." *New York Times*, 15 Mar. 2006, E2.

———. "Princeton to Return Disputed Art to Italy." nytimes.com, 27 Oct. 2007.

Pre-Columbian Monumental, Architectural Sculpture and Murals Act [19 USC §§2091-2095] Regulations: [19 CFR §§12.105-12.109 (1972)]<http://uscode.house.gov/download/pls/19C11.txt>.

Princeton University. "Princeton University Art Museum and Italy Sign Agreement over Antiquities." Media-Newswire.com, 1 Nov. 2007. 22 Dec. 2010<http://media-newswire.com/release_1056887.html>.

Prott, Lyndel V., and Patrick J. O'Keefe. *Handbook of National Regulations Concerning the Export of Cultural Property*. Sydney, Australia: UNESCO, 1988.

Register of Professional Archaeologists. "Code of Conduct and Standards of Research Performance." 7 Aug. 2010<http://www.rpanet.org/displaycommon.cfm?an=1&subarticlenbr=3>.

Renfrew, Colin. *Loot, Legitimacy and Ownership: The Ethical Crisis in Archaeology*. Amsterdam: Joh. Ensched, 1999.

Roberts, Paul. "Barriers or Bridges? Museums and Acquisitions." In *Who Owns Objects? The Ethics and Politics of Collecting Cultural Artefacts, Proceedings for the First St Cross—All Souls Seminar Series and Workshop, Oxford, October–December 2004*, edited by E. Robson, L. Treadwell, and C. Gosden, 47–59. Oxford, UK: Oxbow Books, 2006.

Rose, Mark. "Special Report: Church Treasures of Cyprus." *Archeology* 51 (July/Aug. 1998): 4.

Saving Antiquities for Everyone. 14 Feb. 2011<http://www.savingantiquities.org>.

Simmons, John. *Things Great and Small: Collections Management Policies*. Washington, DC: American Association of Museums, 2006.

Slayman, Andrew L. "Geneva Seizure." Archaeology. 14 Sept. 1998. 8 Jan. 2011<http://www.archaeology.org/online/features/geneva/index.html>.

Smith, George S., and John E. Ehrehard. *Protecting the Past*. National Park Service Southeast Archeological Center, 3 Aug. 2000. 7 Aug. 2010.<http://www.cr.nps.gov/seac/protecting/>.

Smithsonian Institution Archives, National Collections Program. "Chapter 21, Specific Legal Issues, Cultural Property." Smithsonian Directive (SD) 600: Collections Management Implementation Manual (Draft). Washington, DC: Smithsonian Institution, 22 Oct. 2003, 226–232.

Stuart, George E. "Conclusion: Working Together to Preserve Our Past." In *The Ethics of Collecting Cultural Property: Whose Culture? Whose Property?*, 2nd ed., edited by Phyllis Mauch Messenger, 243–251. Albuquerque: University of New Mexico Press, 1999.

Thomas, David A. "Adverse Possession: Acquiring Title to Stolen Personal Property." *Probate & Property* 10 (Mar./Apr. 1996), 12.

Todeschini, Cecilia, and Peter Watson. *Medici Conspiracy: The Illicit Journey of Looted Antiquities—From Italy's Tomb Raiders to the World's Greatest Museums*. New York: Public Affairs, 2006.

Trace. 30 Jan. 2011<www.trace.com/>.

Treaty of Cooperation between the United States of America and the United Mexican States Providing for the Recovery and Return of Stolen Archaeological, Historical, and Cultural Properties. 17 July 1970 (22 U.S.T. 494. Article 1).

United Kingdom Department for Culture, Media and Sport. *Combating Illicit Trade: Due Diligence Guidelines for Museums, Libraries and Archives on Collecting and Borrowing Cultural Material*. London: Crown Copyright: October 2005. 7 Feb. 2011<http://www.culture.gov.uk/Reference_library/Publications/archive_2005/illicit_trade.htm>.

United Kingdom Museums, Libraries & Archives Council. "Buying from On-Line Sources." Cultural Property Advice. 2006. 7 Feb. 2011<http://www.culturalproperty-advice.gov.uk/>.

———. "Acceptable Evidence for Due Diligence." Cultural Property Advice. 2006. 7 Jan. 2011<http://www.culturalpropertyadvice.gov.uk>.

United Nations Educational, Scientific, and Social Organization. *The UNESCO Convention on the Means of Prohibiting the Illicit Import, Export, and Transfer of Ownership of Cultural Property*. Geneva: UNESCO, 1970.

———. The Collection of Legislative Texts Concerning the Protection of Movable Cultural Property 1985–1988<http://unesdoc.unesco.org/images/0007/000785/078538eo.pdf>.

United States Department of Homeland Security, Customs and Border Protection. What Every Member of the Trade Community Should Know about Works of Art, Collector's Pieces, Antiques, and Other Cultural Property. May 2006. 14 Feb. 2011<http://www.cbp.gov/linkhandler/cgov/trade/legal/informed_compliance_pubs/icp061.ctt/icp061.pdf>.

———.Entry Summary (CBP Form 7501). June 2009. 19 Nov. 2010.<http://forms.cbp.gov/pdf/CBP_Form_7501.pdf>.

———. Prohibited and Restricted Items. 17 Dec. 2010. 11 Feb. 2011<http://www.cbp.gov/xp/cgov/travel/vacation/kbyg/prohibited_restricted.xml>.

———. Department of the Interior. National Park Service. Native American Graves Protection and Repatriation Act. 14 Feb. 2011<http://www.cr.nps.gov/nagpra/>.

———. Archaeology Program. 14 Feb. 2011<http://www.nps.gov/archeology/>.

———. Cultural Resources Program. *Federal Historic Preservation Laws*. Washington, DC, 1993.

———. NAGPRA Glossary. 14 Feb. 2011<http://www.cr.nps.gov/nagpra/TRAINING/GLOSSARY.HTM>.

———. Office of the Secretary. "Curation of Federally-Owned and Administered Archaeological Collections." Federal Register. 36 CFR Part 79. 37670: 12 Sept. 1990.

———. Department of the Treasury. Office of Foreign Assets Control. Sanctions Programs. 1 Mar. 2011. 4 Mar. 2011<http://www.ustreas.gov/offices/enforcement/ofac/programs/index.shtml>.

United States Department of Homeland Security, Customs and Border Protection. State Department, Bureau of Educational and Cultural Affairs. Chart of Current and Expired Import Restrictions under the Convention on Cultural Property Implementation Act. 17 Nov. 2010<http://exchanges.state.gov/heritage/culprop/chart2.pdf>.

Urice, Stephen K. "Antiquities as Cultural Property: Dealing with the Past, Looking to the Future—An Introduction." *Course of Studies Materials: Legal Problems of Museum Administration*. Philadelphia: American Law Institute and American Bar Association, 2007.

———. "Between Rocks and Hard Places: Unprovenanced Antiquities and the National Stolen Property Act." *New Mexico Law Review* 40 (Winter 2010): 123–161. http://lawlibrary.unm.edu/nmlr/40/1/06_urice_between.pdf (15 Feb. 2011).

U.S. v. An Antique Platter of Gold, 991 F. Supp. 222 (S.D.N.Y. 1997) aff'd, 184 F. 3d 131 (2d Cir. 1999).

U.S. v. An Archaic Etruscan Pottery Ceremonial Vase c. Late 7th Century, B.C., and a Set of Rare Villanovan and Archaic Etruscan Blackware with Buchero and Impasto Ware, c. 8th–7th Century, B.C., Located at Antiquarium, Ltd., 948 Madison Avenue, New York, NY., 10021, No. 96 Civ. 9437 (S.D.N.Y. 24 Mar. 1997).

U.S. v. Barchitta, No. 1:03-cr-00437 (E.D. Va. consent order of forfeiture entered 24 Sept. 2003).

U.S. v. Gerber, 999 F. 2d 1112, 1114 (7th Cir. 1993).

U.S. v. Hollinshead, 495 F.2d 1154 (9th Cir. 1974).

U.S. v. McClain, 545 F.2nd 988 (5th Cir. 1977), and *U. S. v. McClain*, 593 F.2nd 658 (5th Cir. 1979).

U.S. v. Schultz, 333 F.3rd 395 (2nd Cir. 2002). Cert. denied. *Schultz v. U.S.*, 540 U.S.1106. 157 L.Ed. 2nd 891. 124 S. Ct. 1051 (2004).

Vitale, Katherine D. "The War on Antiquities: United States Law and Foreign Cultural Property." *Notre Dame Law Review* 84 (2009)<http://papers.ssrn.com/sol3/papers.cfm?abstract_id=1346575>.

Watson, Rubie. "Culturally Sensitive Collections: A Museum Perspective." In *Stewards of the Sacred*, edited by Lawrence E. Sullivan and Alison Edwards, 113–122. Washington, DC and Cambridge, MA: American Association of Museums and Harvard University Center for the Study of World Religions, 2004.

Weil, Stephen E. "Collecting Then, Collecting Today: What's the Difference?" In *Reinventing the Museum: Historical and Contemporary Perspectives on the Paradigm Shift*, edited by Gail Anderson, 284–291. Walnut Creek, CA: AltaMira Press, 2004.

———. "From Being *about* Something to Being *for* Somebody: The Ongoing Transformation of the American Museum." *Daedalus*. Summer 1999: 229–258.

Wyatt, Edward. "Papers Show Wider Focus in Inquiry of Artifacts." nytimes.com, 30 Jan. 2008. 3 Feb. 2008<http://www.nytimes.com/2008/01/30/us/30 museum.html?scp=1&sq=Papers+Show+Wider+Focus+in+Inquiry+of+Artifacts&st=nyt>.

Index

R

S

About the Author

Aimée Taberner received her Master's Degree in Museum Studies, with distinction, from Harvard University Extension, and her Bachelor's Degree in Art History from the University of Massachusetts, Amherst. She has passionately pursued the topics of archaeology, fine arts, historic preservation, and cultural property law, both academically and professionally. She serves on the board of the New England Chapter of the Society of Architectural Historians, and is the co-chair of the Board of Trustees for the Cyrus E. Dallin Art Museum in Arlington, Massachusetts.

Aimée is a strong supporter of preservation and conservation initiatives, both for cultural and environmental resources. A believer in the importance of educating the public regarding the value of archaeological resources, she coordinated the Archaeology Week educational programs while working at the Massachusetts Historical Commission and has volunteered on several archaeological investigations. An internship at the Harvard University Peabody Museum for Archaeology and Ethnology resulted in a draft policy intended to aid in operationalizing the decision-making process for the acquisition of cultural property and archaeological material. This research was further developed under the direction of faculty at Harvard Law School and then shared at the 2008 AAM Annual Conference.

Her problem-solving and project management skills are well utilized at Harvard University's Graduate School of Design where she plays a central role in course planning and cross-departmental academic initiatives. While a pragmatic problem solver by profession, she is at heart an idealist who firmly believes in the positive role that all humanity can play in achieving a better world through collaboration, compassion, and communication. She hopes this publication makes a modest contribution to this broader goal and is of assistance to those working with those precious, nonrenewable resources that are, or may someday be, within museum collections.